Adjusting the fine focus I saw that they were women, working with large-spaded hoes.

I swept the field and saw a hut. Sitting outside it were two old men, watching the women work. They, too, were wearing the indigenous white dress of the peasant.

Picking up the phone I located Leggy at the infantry command post.

'Can you come round here? I've sighted some people working in a rice field three or four miles away.'

Leggy arrived within minutes. His shirt was sweat-soaked under the armpits and his breath stank of whisky. Binoculars swung from his neck.

'Whereabouts?' he puffed.

I told him as I was drawing the new-found territory on the panorama board. He looked through the donkey's ears, then focused his own binoculars.

'Get the 25-pounders,' he ordered. 'They should be in range.'

'But they are *women*!' I protested.

'Kingsland,' he said, 'they are *enemy*.' He spoke slowly and with emphasis. 'They could have anything hidden in that hut.' Then his tone relaxed. 'Besides, there's nothing else to shoot at! Now be a good lad and get the guns on the phone. It will be good practice for you.'

In Quest of Glory

Gerald Kingsland

NEW ENGLISH LIBRARY
Hodder and Stoughton

Printed and bound in Great
Britain for Hodder and
Stoughton Paperbacks, a
division of Hodder and
Stoughton Ltd., Mill Road,
Dunton Green, Sevenoaks, Kent
TN13 2YA. (Editorial Office: 47
Bedford Square, London WC1B
3DP) by Clays Ltd, St Ives plc

British Library C.I.P.

Kingsland, Gerald
  In quest of glory.
  1. Korean War – Biographies
  I. Title
  951.9042092

  ISBN 0-450-42473-6

For Captain Legg and Stan, and all men of the Korean Battery of Mortars – those anonymous nomads of the front line whose guts and determination helped win glory for the regiments and units they supported. They stuck it out through all attacks, even when successive regiments came and went. And many laid down their lives.

Foreword

This book is not a historian's impersonal account of the Korean War. It is the intimate, true story of my experience of it. I was a Forward Observer for thirteen shell-torn and rat-infested months until the peace treaty was signed, and I saw action at every forward observation post on the Commonwealth front and at two on the American front.

Although I did write some form of manuscript nearly twenty years ago when I had no experience as an author, this book is also written from a memory almost twice as old. Therefore, while it is possible that a particular hill was not occupied by a particular unit at the time suggested, the facts remain that the unit *was* on that particular hill, that I was with that unit, and while there the incidents described *did* take place there.

Also I regret to say that time has erased from my memory many names; and when I have, of necessity, substituted a name, that person will readily be able to identify himself.

I was an ordinary soldier with scant knowledge of the tactical strategy or Intelligence of war. Like many other young men who fought in Korea I had little idea of where I was half the time and had only vague conceptions of what the fighting was about. I simply obeyed orders.

Now, drawing on that earlier manuscript and the memories indelibly printed in my mind, I have set out to show the crudity and vulgarity of war, how easily it can reduce a man to animal level.

Above all, I wish to show what war is really like: a bloody waste of time and lives, especially as today, despite what we endured and the many young men who valiantly died, I see in the news that the political situation in Korea is much the same as it was then.

There is another reason – apart from the normal egotistical autobiographical one – why I have written this book: to answer the oft-asked questions of why I am as I am: recalcitrant, irresponsible and irreligious; and why I wanted to be Robinson Crusoe, in search of something more than the secure mundane.

I hope this book will give some of the answers, especially to the two daughters I abandoned when they were very young.

Gerald Kingsland
Chile

Illustrations

Acknowledgment:

All pictures by kind permission of the Imperial War Museum

1

'While your record of whoring and drunken brawling has been barely acceptable,' said the Airborne commanding officer, 'and while the "borrowing" of a car to get back to barracks could, at the extreme, be described as initiative, crashing the blasted car and being caught by the police is insufferable. And you've crashed two cars in four months and been caught by the police both times! It was an embarrassment having to send one of my officers to a magistrates' court to get you off the hook on *one* occasion, let alone two. I have no alternative. I am returning you to the Royal Artillery, the regiment in which you first enlisted.'

It was January 1952 and I was twenty-one. I had served nearly three years as a paratrooper in the Royal Airborne Artillery, a regiment within the Independent Parachute Brigade. In those days a person had to enlist in another regiment first to do 'square bashing' and training before being able to volunteer for the Paras. Only infantry personnel were eligible to join the Parachute Regiment. The rest of us kept our original regiments' specialist identities – e.g. Royal Airborne Engineers – wore the red beret, Pegasus and parachutist's wings, and were assigned to one of the Parachute Regiment's three battalions. As an anti-tank man I was with the Third Battalion.

'Sir!' I blurted. 'I wish to volunteer for Korea.'

'I'm sorry, but we have no airborne unit out there that I can transfer you to. I told you that a year ago. But you'll be able to do so through the ordinary artillery. March out!'

I was waiting to be posted when I heard that the SAS had been re-formed, with the added title 'Malayan Scouts', to try to do something about the steady slaughter of British soldiers in the Malayan jungle. A major was at Parachute

1

Brigade Headquarters, Maida Barracks, Aldershot, looking for volunteers. He sounded to me like a God-sent opportunity. With the adventure, action and added kudos that the new SAS was offering, I felt sure that, at last, I would get out from under the shadow of my two elder brothers' glory. It was a much better proposition than Korea. After all, SAS men were known as 'Death or Glory Boys'!

The SAS major tut-tutted a few times as he read my conduct sheet. When he raised his head his pale-blue eyes were piercing:

'So, the Paras consider you to be "undesirable", eh? That is how they put it. You've been rather naughty, getting caught by the police. One might even say, slipshod. Drunk at the time?'

'No, sir. I haven't passed my driving test yet.'

I thought I detected a flicker of a smile raise the corners of his mouth. 'Good!' he said, brightly, to my surprise and relief. 'You seem to be the sort of chap we're looking for.'

'Thank you, sir!' I said, gustily.

The blue eyes still held mine. 'Why do you want to join the SAS, Kingsland?'

Truthfully, I told him. 'One of my brothers was on submarines during the war and the other was a Pathfinder. I feel a need to prove that I'm as good, if not better, than they were.'

'I see,' he said, quietly, and wrote rapidly on a notepad. Then he tossed his pen on to the desk, sat back and became affably conspiratorial:

'We have come up with a new idea for training soldiers for jungle warfare – letting them stalk each other with powerful air rifles. Very painful if a slug hits you. Makes you more careful the next time.' He smiled. I smiled back. He referred to my papers again. 'And I see you're an excellent shot. You did a course at the Larkhill School of Ballistics. Good. By the way, you'll be jumping out of helicopters not aeroplanes. Any objection?'

'None at all, sir!'

'Now then, I see you've only two years, two months left to serve. If you want to come with me you'll have to sign on for two more years, making your contract seven with the Colours and five with the Reserve. This tour of duty, as in the Paras, is for three years minimum, otherwise it wouldn't be worth the transportation and training of you.'

My heart sank but I kept a brave face. 'I would like to talk it over with my mother, sir. She is a widow and over fifty.'

'I quite understand. Talk it over with your mother. You have a week to decide. I'll still be here.'

As I'd anticipated, my mother's tearful outburst was seemingly incessant when I told her what I wanted to do. After her initial wail of 'You can't do this thing to me, Gerald. Look how terrible the war years were for me,' she went into a long history, as she had often done, of what she had endured.

Eldest son, Murray, had two destroyers, the *Hyperion* and the *Imperial*, sunk under him in the Mediterranean. Fifteen officers and men, including Murray, were left on board the bomb-crippled *Imperial* to get her to safety. But she was too far gone and continually under bombardment, so they scuttled her. For that action, Murray received the Distinguished Service Order. After that he manned the Bofors on the Rock of Gibraltar during its worst raids by German aircraft, and received another medal. Then he was put on submarines. As my father jokingly said: 'The Admiralty probably thinks he'll be safer under the water!'

Second son, Geoffrey, 'not content with being an ordinary soldier', as Mum often moaned, joined the Paras and almost died of pneumonia during the harsh Commando training course in the Ben Nevis range in Scotland, where today stands a monument to the Commando who endured terrible hardship. Then he became a Pathfinder – a paratrooper who goes in first to prepare the DZ (Dropping Zone) – in readiness for the D-Day landings in France.

'Those years, with all the anxiety and the dread of a black-edged telegram, were terrible for me,' my mother's wailing continued. 'And just when the war was over and everything was peaceful once more, your father died. It was cruel – cruel – of you to have gone off, jumping out of aeroplanes when I needed you most. Why couldn't you have

3

stayed on the farm where you belonged? Your father was hardly cold in his grave. Now Murray's married, Geoffrey soon will be and I'll be all alone. Please don't sign on, Gerald, please, I beg of you.'

Her outburst – although I had expected it – made me angry. But the anger quickly subsided and guilt engulfed me. I loved her very much. I put my arms around her and she hugged me.

'Mum,' I said, softly, into her greying hair, 'can't you see how I feel? Always, you and Dad were boasting about Murray and Geoff. Don't you understand what I have to compete with?' I felt her tense and I held her tighter. 'Listen to me. I was nothing and all I could hear were your praises of Murray and Geoff. I was a farm labourer until I joined the Paras – a hick, that's what Murray called me. He even introduced me to Joan as such.'

'You *wanted* to work on a farm,' she accused me, the words partly muffled by the shoulder of my tunic. 'You've always done what *you* wanted. You tore off from school like a mad thing when you were fourteen. If you'd stayed on, the headmaster had a good job waiting for you in the Council offices. But, no, you wouldn't be told.'

I relaxed my arms. She pulled her head back and her words became clearer – and sarcastic: 'And how long did you stick to farming? Five years! Pah! It nearly broke my heart when you told me you had joined up.'

'It suddenly occurred to me that there was something more to life than looking at the backsides of two horses pulling a plough,' I said, with an attempt at humour, which she ignored. 'Oh, Mum, I just *had* to join the Paras – I certainly didn't want to go on submarines. I wanted some glory, too – I still do. I want to prove myself.'

Indignation arose immediately and she pushed me away from her. 'No one has to prove himself! And I'm sick of your glory and honour. They do no one any good when you're dead. And no one will thank you for it.' The tears flooded again. 'I'm telling you, Gerald,' she sobbed, 'I'll go out of my mind if you join the SAS – probably put my head in the gas oven.'

4

'All right, Mum, all right,' I soothed her. 'Don't say any more. I promise I won't sign on.'

The tears stopped instantly. She dried her face with a tea towel. 'Now, you sit yourself down at the table and I'll get you a nice tea. I've a lovely piece of ham.'

The disappointment within me was very deep. I deemed it wise to say nothing about my being 'undesirable' or about the Korean war. Saying I had leave only for the weekend, I caught a train from Aylesbury on the Sunday to go to Dorset to see Sylvia. She was another reason why I wanted to be a hero. Tall, slim and raven-haired, Sylvia was nineteen and resembled a photo of my mother taken at that age.

'I know how you feel,' she said, 'but, in a way, I am pleased about what's happened, and that you're out of the Paras. And I can see your mother's point of view about the SAS. When Geoff marries she will only have you left. And what about me? It won't do me any good, either, if you get yourself killed. Malaya is an awful long way away, and we might not see each other for three whole years! Probably never! If only you didn't have this complex about glory and such a strange wildness within you. It must be your red hair.' She ran her fingers through it and kissed me.

Although still feeling disappointed, I cheered up after hearing her words. Also, there were five nights and four days of her company to enjoy.

I had known Sylvia for more than a year, since a few months after the Paras were recalled from Germany. In Germany I had teamed up with her brother, 'Pug', a physical-training instructor. It was he who told me that after working for five years as a farm labourer, I was muscle-bound. He suggested I should box for the Regiment and he would be my trainer. He said it would make my muscles supple; get rid of some of my restless aggressiveness, which I didn't realise I had; and it would get both of us off 'bullshit' parades and guard duty!

I fought six welter-weight bouts and won them all. The second was the most memorable, when we boxed the 1st Royal Tank Regiment. One never saw one's opponent until entering the ring.

'I don't want to frighten you, Kingy,' said Pug, as our sergeant-major was lacing up my gloves, 'but I've just seen your opponent. His knuckles brush the sides of his knees when he walks! I'm not kidding!'

The sergeant-major gripped my gloves. 'Courage, man, courage,' he comforted me. 'Remember, you're in the élite. A packet of Player's for you if you knock the bastard out cold. We're down on points.'

My opponent was big but mostly bone – and without strategy. I felled him in the second round – and I never did get my cigarettes!

It was Pug, too, who started up a hockey team. I played outside-left. When we decided we were ready to challenge the world, we flung down the gauntlet to a girls' convent school in Hamelin, where according to the classic poem, 'the River Weser runs deep and wide'.

'My God,' puffed Pug, after the first fifteen minutes, 'these bitches can really run – faster than the bloody river!'

Back in barracks everyone wanted to know how we'd fared.

'Eleven each,' we replied, 'one for each player on their side! Even their goalie came out to score!'

Our only excuse was that we had been distracted by flashing white thighs and silky knickers. After that, the hockey project was abandoned.

I had warmed to Pug because he was a lot like me – devil-may-care, a hater of bullshit and not too fond of discipline. Many times when our 'stick' of twenty paratroopers jumped from a Dakota aircraft, nineteen of us would be facing one way and he would be facing the other.

'Kingy!' he would yell to me, waving wildly with both hands, and the wind would blow him right off course. I would take one hand off the guide lines and wave back.

'Silence in the air! Control those rigging lines, man!' a stern voice would boom at him through a megaphone on the ground. Invariably, Pug would miss the DZ completely and receive a double reprimand for speaking in the air as well.

We'd had our fair share of street and café fights in Germany – during one skirmish in Hamburg, another Para who

6

was with us was shot clean through the left buttock by a Military Policeman – but England seemed to be worse.

Pubs, especially those in London, were very different from what they are today. Unaccompanied women were mostly whores or prostitutes, and bars were pretty much a man's domain. The Red Beret courted trouble. Not many publicans liked us. Often when Pug and I entered a bar we'd hear someone sneer, with the Dutch courage inside him: 'Bloody paratroopers – they think they're tough', or 'They're just living on dead men's glory'. Sometimes we could ignore it. Other times we were forced not to. A bottle or beer glass would be broken, and Pug and I had to use all we'd learned about unarmed combat.

But we were definitely the culprits where American paratroopers were concerned. We detested their boasting. At that time the British paratrooper jumped with only one 'chute. The Americans used an emergency 'chute as well. Pug and I could never resist the temptation to tell them they were 'big cissies' when we heard them bragging to English tarts.

Then one weekend Pug said to me: 'Come home with me and meet my sister. I'm sure she'd like you. We live near Bridport where there's a nice little pub and it's always peaceful and quiet.'

I fell head over heels in love the instant I saw Sylvia. Every chance I had I went to Bridport. Sometimes she would travel to her married sister's house in Woolwich for a romantic weekend. But many weekends I couldn't be with her, and almost always I got into trouble. I never told her, but Pug was with me on that last occasion.

After I had hot-wired a selected car, the engine took a while to start, and lights came on in the owner's house. When the engine finally fired, I accelerated fast. Rounding a bend I skidded sideways into a stationary steam-roller!

'What a fucking stupid place to leave a steam-roller!' I yelled, and kept on going. Headlights were soon flashing in my driving mirror and we heard the clang of a police car's bell close behind. I put my foot down even more. An S-bend came up. I had managed to get round the first half of the S when a large tree got in the way.

7

The doors of the car opened forwards and Pug, knowing my capabilities as a driver, held his door partly open in anticipation. The head-on impact with the tree sent him hurtling through the door. He did a parachutist's roll, regained his feet and disappeared into the night. My door was jammed shut by the impact with the steam-roller. The men in blue grabbed me as I was trying to clamber over the gear lever and hand brake.

The station sergeant was red-faced, bull-necked and huge-bellied. 'I want the name of the other paratrooper,' he demanded.

'Piss off!' I said with drunken bravado.

His fist hit me behind the right ear and sent me flying off the chair. He was about to hit me again when an attractive policewoman entered the room. She took over and bathed the cut lip I'd received in the crash.

'Why does a nice-looking young boy like you have to do this sort of thing?' she said, with a sigh. 'Do you want to tell me the other paratrooper's name?' Another sigh. 'No, I can see you don't.'

When I told the SAS major of my decision not to sign on, I was sent to a specialist mortar battery in Germany. I was allowed to wear my paratrooper wings on my right shoulder and to wear my Red Beret – an honour that only a court-martial could take from me. I was welcomed in my capacity as a signals instructor and given back my two stripes. I passed a driving test and did a course as a TARA – Technical Assistant, Royal Artillery – with accompanying courses in sound detection.

I shared a room in the comfortable barracks with a young, teetotal conscript who was studying Greek for Oxford University entrance. I read Homer's *Odyssey* and *Iliad* and thoroughly enjoyed them. They were full of heroes like I wanted to be. Then I studied Greek mythology and memorised the family tree of the gods, commencing with Zeus and Hera. Suddenly, I found I loved words and began reading, like a book, the *Concise Oxford Dictionary*. And I would show off new words in my letters to Sylvia.

8

I just wanted to fill my head, for always churning inside me was the dilemma: to go or not to go to Korea. Every time when I was about to volunteer, a letter would arrive from Sylvia or Mum.

For two months – apart from an occasional fight with Krauts who claimed, probably rightly so, that the British had killed their parents – I was of unblemished character. Then came the night of the barracks dance.

Her name was Ilse and she had legs as shapely as Sylvia's and encased in the sheerest of nylon stockings. A lack of conscience, sponsored by lust, prompted me to take her home. I also ignored the fact that a curfew was in force. With the memory of the warmth of her delicious stockinged thighs and what lay between, I staggered from her house at six o'clock in the morning – straight into the arms of two Military Policemen!

The battery commanding officer just didn't want such an irresponsible person in his specialist unit. He told me so in no uncertain terms, adding that a curfew charge brought by the Military Police was very serious.

'You are not suited to life as a peacetime soldier, Kingsland – you need action. So I've volunteered you for Korea. An entire mortar battery was wiped out with the Gloucesters last year and they still need men for the new battery. You'll do nicely. Get your gear together. March out!'

I couldn't believe my luck, and the onus of decision wasn't mine, after all! Three cheers for Ilse. Thanks to her, I was going. It occurred to me that my wayward ways had, at last, paid off.

Even today, though, I still wonder what I would be doing now had I not been tempted by Ilse or if I had ignored my mother's plea and joined the SAS. As she always told me when I was a boy: 'Life's road is full of turnings – and the one you take is predetermined. Everyone is born to die, and only God knows how long or short your road to the grave will be.'

Many times have I wished I could go up all the turnings – just to have a look!

With each mile that the train drew closer to Aylesbury,

9

I more and more dreaded Mum's reaction, though I tried to comfort myself that it shouldn't be too bad. After all, I hadn't increased the length of time I had to serve. But she ranted and raved like a mad thing.

'You're not going!' she stormed. 'I'll write to the Army. I'll hide you! You're not going!'

'Don't be silly, Mum,' said Geoff. 'He's under Active Service orders. They'd probably shoot him if he deserted now.'

'I don't care,' she cried, irrationally. 'He'll be killed! I know he will. It's too much to ask of God that three sons should survive a war. In my heart I know it will be God's wish to take him. He is a third son. Only yesterday I saw a terrible picture in the tea leaves at the bottom of my cup.'

Since the age of thirteen I'd not had much time for God. As a boy, though, on a remote Buckinghamshire farm, I had been steeped in my mother's morbidity over death and her beliefs and superstitions born of the Church, ignorance and candlelight: bad luck would be sure to come if you gathered firewood, or cut your fingernails on a Sunday. Looking at a new moon over your left shoulder was positively lethal. A person could hardly move without some awful portent occurring – you had to be on your guard against black cats, cracked or broken mirrors, single magpies, crossed knives on the table, ladders and spilt salt, to name a few things. Her indoctrinations still clung even though I had tried to shrug them off.

Every day of my embarkation leave she would suddenly burst into tears, saying she'd seen another sign that I was going to my death. Thankfully, I had again told her a lie – that I only had one week left. I wanted the other week with Sylvia; and Mum's daily insistence that I would be killed was telling on my morale.

By the time it came to say goodbye I felt wretched and convinced that I was, in fact, going to my death. Mum, Geoff and our Alsatian, Tania, all came to Aylesbury station to see me off.

'Look after yourself,' said Geoff, gruffly. 'And remember, keep your head down.'

As the train pulled away, Tania began barking, Mum had her face buried in a large handkerchief and Geoffrey waved.

Tears tried to emerge from my eyes, but failed. How strange, I thought, with my mother's induced premonition within me that I would never see them again, my main grief was for Tania.

Sylvia would just not believe I had not volunteered for Korea, and I sensed something different about her.

'You know what I think about war,' she said. 'It's hateful. And how many times have I told you to forget your brothers and forget war.'

The hurt over my going eased but never fully died. Even so, like sporadic shafts of sunshine through dark, ominous cloud, our love lightened our depression; but always the looming end of the week hung over our happy moments like the Sword of Damocles. Then the cobweb snapped – a train, resembling an evil, emotionless, mythological caterpillar, was waiting to swallow me and take me out of her life.

'I'm not going to cry,' she said, flatly, though her eyes were swimming. 'See. I'm not.' Red lipstick framed her white teeth for a brave smile. We held each other tightly.

'I love you,' she choked. 'Oh, why did you have to do this? I just hope you find your glory. Please come back. I'll write you every week.'

I cried like a baby in one of the train's lavatories for part of that awful journey to London, sitting on the hard seat and mournfully calling her name.

2

'I say!' said an awfully-awfully voice at my right shoulder. 'Can you possibly tell me if I'm on the right boat for Jamaica? Such *terrible* confusion at Liverpool!'

I was standing alone, leaning on the troopship's rail and staring moodily at the wake now that England had dropped from sight. The humour of the remark cut across my despondent reverie. I turned and took in the upturned wings of the SAS parachutist's badge sitting above three rows of medals and campaign ribbons.

'A Caribbean cruise would be pretty good,' I said, laughing.

'I saw your Red Beret,' he went on, in a normal voice, 'and thought, thank Christ I won't have to spend all my time on this arsehole of a tub with lesser beings.' He proffered his hand. 'People call me Jungle because they say I'm not quite right in the head.'

I shook his hand, warmly. He had a lopsided grin, a casual stance, and he reminded me of Murray. 'People call me Kingy,' I said. 'I take it you're on the way to Malaya?'

'Good lord, no!' the awfully-awfully voice came again. 'Much too long in the tooth, doncha know, for the jolly old "Who Dares Wins" motto, and playing silly buggers in the jungle doesn't appeal, what?' He reverted to his normal voice. 'The delights of Pusan await me. You, too?'

'Yep. I'm earmarked for the mortars.'

'Sharp end stuff. I've got me a nice safe job with the 25-pounders. I only have to do a year out there, then it's Hong Kong for me in married quarters to finish my time.' He produced a photo of an attractive woman and a little boy and girl. 'They're really looking forward to Hong Kong.'

In turn, I showed him a photo of Sylvia. It was good

12

to have found someone I could talk to, and someone I respected. I told him of the roundabout way I had come to be on my way to Korea.

'Do you think it's wrong of me to have this bee in my bonnet about glory?' I asked.

He shook his head. 'The war caused – and left – a lot of young men like you. Come on! Let's have a beer. It must be opening time.'

When we were sitting comfortably in the spacious 'Other Ranks' bar, he said: 'Did you know that this tub, the *Halladale*, was originally built as one of Hitler's "Strength Through Joy" boats? He would pack them with selected blue-eyed, fair-haired, young men and women and send them up into the Baltic to procreate a pure Aryan race.' Jungle laughed. 'Think of all the fucking that went on on board this tub – and here we sit in celibacy! It's enough to make your eyes water.'

His voice became serious. 'Hitler really had a thing about a pure race – that's why he was down on the Jews. I speak fluent German and I read a manifesto of his, written in 1921. Even then he was calling the Jews the scum of the earth.'

'Those concentration camps were diabolical, weren't they?' I said. 'I went to Belsen in 1949, just to have a look, and the crematorium ashes still reeked of burnt pork if you moved them with your foot.'

We were silent for a while. Then I asked: 'What was your main task in the war, Jungle? Or is that a trade secret?'

'Saboteur,' he said, putting his pint on the table. 'And do you know, Kingy, the one thing I regret is that I caused the deaths of many innocent Frenchmen. I would be parachuted into France to blow up a train, tunnel or bridge. Then I would have to make my own way to the coast where a submarine would be waiting at a scheduled time. And, because of what I had done, the Germans would line up a few people from a near-by village and shoot them. That has always played on my mind.'

Jungle was quartered in another part of the troopship. Two afternoons later, as we were passing through the Straits of Gibraltar, he again found me at the rail. I was deep

13

in thought again, but this time about Murray's wartime experience on the Rock and the fact that I was seeing Africa for the first time. Hitherto, it had been a country only in geography books or films, as were all the countries we were to pass or visit.

'I know the procedure on these sort of tubs,' he told me. 'Cretinous officers will marshal us into playing deck-games and attending lectures and parades. For'ard – and I use the nautical term – there is a large, deep coil of rope in which two bodies could become lost – if you get my drift.'

And to that coil of rope, where no one ever found us, we would repair whenever we had no wish to participate in something or other; and there, like the Walrus, we would 'talk of many things'. The more I knew him, the more I liked him and the more I confided in him.

After we had passed the giant statue of Ferdinand de Lesseps, standing on a pedestal of concrete in the sea at the mouth of the Suez Canal, called in at Aden and were making our way down the Red Sea, I said to him: 'Well, I'm certainly seeing the world at the Army's expense – I just hope it's not at the expense of my life!'

He looked at me closely. Then I was telling him about the terrible premonition I had, and how my mother's intuition had bitten into me.

'That's bad about your mother,' he said. 'Look, how many jumps did you make?'

'Twenty-four. Why?'

'And I bet that always at the back of your mind was a teeny little nagging doubt that the bloody parachute wouldn't open. Right?'

'Right.'

'Therefore, you could say that every one of those doubts was a premonition. You've had twenty-four and you're still alive. *Ergo*, premonitions are meaningless.'

Before I could answer, he went on: 'I don't think it's natural not to have them. For me – now – there's a doubt that I won't make it to Hong Kong. Every time I went into action I had a premonition. In fact, the more times I went in, the more I thought that the law of averages was bound to catch up with me!'

'But what about these so-called fearless hard men that you see in American war films and Westerns?' I wanted to know.

'Crap!' he said. 'Utter crap! Hard men cannot be rational – to be without fear, you must have the crazed mentality of a kamikaze pilot, or be drunk, have vengeance in your heart, have a death wish or be a psychopath. And in my book an action without fear is not bravery. When you were clamouring for your glory you were irrational – without fear. Now you are facing the reality of what you wanted and you've become normal and rational again – with fear!'

His seriousness dissolved. He put on his awfully-awfully voice. 'Dashed good to meet a rational chap, what?'

As the *Halladale* was lazing her way through the sun-hazed Indian Ocean, and Jungle and I were hiding in our coil of rope, he said: 'Did I ever tell you about the first man I killed?'

'No,' I replied, eager to hear.

He took a deep drag of his cigarette. 'That's another thing that always stays in my mind. I was your age. Before I joined the SAS I was in the British Expeditionary Force that first went to France. That was a fucking disaster. I'll always remember the hell of Dunkirk. Anyway, I was crawling round this rock, with an automatic pistol in my right hand. Suddenly, I came face-to-face with a Kraut crawling round from the other side. He had his rifle in his hand, using it like a ski runner. It was just shit-scaredness that made me squeeze the trigger. And I just kept it held back until his face and head disintegrated and the magazine was empty.'

He puffed on his cigarette a few more times. Then he turned on his elbow to face me. 'The point is, Kingy,' he said, with emphasis in his voice, 'in that split-second before I squeezed the trigger, I saw a face – a human face – like yours – like anybody's; and it was a face that I knew I could be friends with – like I am with you. And, more important, I knew he wanted to be friends with me! He wouldn't have killed me. I knew that! But the fright

15

within me just made me squeeze that trigger – and keep on squeezing it.

'I just lay there for a while, stupefied and wanting to be sick. Then I got up and searched him. And – this is the terrible thing – do you know what I found? A photograph – just like the one I showed you of my wife and kids! And do you know what I did? I cried and cried and cried.'

'Jungle,' I said, caught up in the moment, 'I cried, too, when I said goodbye to Sylvia.'

'Your Sylvia sounds a nice girl,' said Jungle. 'She was quite right when she said that war was hateful.'

As though to answer an unasked question of mine, he said: 'When the war was over, I had no trade. I knew only how to kill and destroy. So I transferred to the Royal Artillery and signed on. And when I leave the Army I'll have a pension to see me all right for the rest of my life. When I die, Angela and the children will be well looked after.'

'Jungle,' I said, 'I really hope you make it to Hong Kong.'

'And I hope you have a nice life with Sylvia,' he said. 'Just concentrate on that. Make her your goal for survival.'

A week or so later we were sitting under a parasol at a table on the immaculately kept lawn of the Galles Face Hotel, Colombo, Ceylon (Sri Lanka), sipping ice-cold beer and watching the Indian Ocean's waves hit and spray over a stone wall at the bottom of the lawn. At that moment, the rest of the world didn't matter.

I interrupted our musings with a laugh as a thought occurred, and he turned to me, enquiringly.

'I just hope my luck in Korea proves better than when I took part in the biggest manoeuvre that Europe has ever known.'

'How come?' he asked.

'We were flown from Histon Airfield, near Cambridge, to drop on Koblenz in Germany to fight the French Army. A 1,000-strong force. I was in the first wave. It was the longest flight in a Dakota I ever made, and I was pretty glad to get out. We came in at operational level – 350 feet. I had just about enough time to get out of my seat strap and lower my kitbag – with a 12-volt battery inside it – when I hit the ground. On the way down I heard the rat-tat-tat of a machine-gun.

'I ditched my parachute quickly and collected my gear to get off the DZ before the next wave's hob-nailed boots and kitbags could knock me flat. Up came an officer with a white armband. "You're dead," he said. "That machine-gun got you. You're out of action for twenty-four hours. There's a nice little café not far from here that will accommodate you."

'Next day I joined the crew of a 6-pounder anti-tank gun. Over the hill came about a dozen French tanks. God, it was frightening. Even on manoeuvres it was frightening to see those monsters rumbling down on us. We started blazing away with our blanks. Then the tank nearest to us opened fire. We felt the wind blast. Up stepped another white-armbanded officer. "You are all dead," he said. "Out of action for twenty-four hours." '

Chuckling, Jungle took another swig of the very potent beer. I followed suit. 'Killed twice in two days does take a bit of beating,' he said.

There was no shore leave at Singapore but launches were waiting when we reached Hong Kong, the world's biggest natural harbour.

'Your future home, Jungle,' I said, excitedly, 'and it's beautiful!'

'I shall make a careful inspection,' he said, as we went down the ship's ladder.

In brilliant, early-morning sunshine, a launch sped us to shore. There we took a ferry to Kowloon where the streets were full of attractive girls in side-split kimonos, showing their stocking-tops and suspenders.

'A cup of tea, I think, don't you?' said Jungle. 'Before my eyes pop out!'

We entered a café down a narrow street. The slim waitress also had a side-split kimono.

'Christ!' I said. 'You can't get away from it!'

'You like tea – all in?' the waitress asked, with a charming mile. 'One dollar each.'

Why not?' said Jungle. 'Hang the expense.'

We sat, sipping our tea, wondering what exotic food was in store, when two girls appeared from a back room, ducked under the tablecloth, which touched the ground, undid our flies and started doing exquisite things!

'My God!' exclaimed Jungle, in his posh voice. 'Tea was never like this with Mater! These Orientals certainly have a different code of ethics, what?'

When we left the café I felt terribly self-conscious and sure that everyone was staring at us because of what had taken place.

'Jungle,' I said, 'I just can't believe it! I think I'll put in for a posting to Hong Kong! It's incredible!'

'Consider it part of life's rich tapestry,' he said.

'You can't eat tapestry,' I retorted, laughing, 'and I'm starving.'

Letters were waiting for us on board the *Halladale*. I had three from Sylvia and two from Mum. Every few days or so I had written paragraphs or poetry to Sylvia, and these I put into an envelope and handed to the mail orderly, together with a hastily scribbled note to Mum.

I read Sylvia's letters every day for the last part of the voyage. Then it was time to say goodbye to Jungle.

The 'Daily Orders' sheet told us we would be docking at Pusan after dark that evening and Jungle and I would be on different sections of the train for Seoul.

'It's taken us six weeks and five days to get here,' he said. 'Perhaps the bloody war is over!'

Once again he proffered his hand. 'Look after yourself, Kingy. Great, knowing you. Love to Sylvia.'

'Yeah. You, too. If I don't see you before, I'll look you and Angela up in Hong Kong on the way back. And don't order any "all-in" teas when she's with you!'

I felt empty and alone without Jungle's company. While the *Halladale*, as we'd jokingly said, surely prompted the song, 'Slow Boat to China', the Seoul train raced through the black night like the clappers. The wooden-slatted carriage seats afforded no comfort, and there was a sickness in my stomach with the surety that I was going to stop the first bullet.

As I degreased, cleaned and loaded my new .303 Lee Enfield rifle, I felt it was a complete waste of time. I would never get the chance to use it. I might just as well leave it greased and unloaded.

Looking at the other ashen-faced young men in the carriage – most of them younger than me and conscripts – I thought 'cannon fodder – that's it. We are all going to be cannon fodder.'

When a bean can suddenly exploded, all of us almost died of fright. Someone had left the unopened can on the burner. The hot beans that splattered me couldn't have felt more like bullets.

After the first yelps, someone laughed with uneasy bravado. Much brave laughter and comments followed. All from bewildered, frightened young men, hurtling through a foreign country we couldn't see through the black carriage windows. A country, I knew full well, that would do much more than bang a can of beans at us.

I remember only two things amid the chaos that seemed to be in Seoul: looking, unsuccessfully, for Jungle and going to the camp cinema to see a film called *Tale of Five Cities*.

I was really enjoying it when, halfway through, the lights went up and a voice commanded: 'All personnel for the mortar battery get aboard the truck outside.'

I really wanted to see the end of that film. To this day, I never have.

3

The detonation of a .303 rifle was shattering to my half-sleeping ears. I felt a bullet thud into my chest and, distantly, I heard a Yorkshire voice exclaim, triumphantly: 'Got the bastard!'

In a split-second, panic-stricken jumble of thoughts on becoming fully awake, I wondered why a bloke from Yorkshire should have wanted to shoot me. There was a heaviness on my sternum and I could feel the heat of escaping blood.

Sick with fear, I raised my head to look. A big, dark-grey, Korean rat was staring at me with blank eyes, its entrails exploded from it.

'Ugh-ugh!' I gagged, and went into a mad scramble to get the bloody thing off my chest.

'That bastard's been looking at me for days.'

This time the voice was much closer. My eyes went to where it came from and took in the grinning countenance of a good-looking, fair-haired, young soldier. He was sitting on a camp-cot less than three feet away, a rifle across his thighs. Fear gave way to fury:

'What the hell did you do that for?' I demanded. 'You could have killed me with a ricochet!'

'Sorry,' came the reply, 'I thought you was asleep.'

'I bloody well was until — ' I began. Then an officer, whose name I remember only as 'Pretty Boy', came flapping through the doorway of the two-man dug-out.

'Who fired a rifle?' he gasped.

'He did,' I said, with a touch of George Washington, and picked the dead rat up by its tail.

'Good heavens!' exclaimed Pretty Boy.

'Damn near killed me,' I went on, maliciously.

Pretty Boy flinched and side-stepped hastily as I tossed

the dead rat past him and out through the door. He turned to the soldier and asked, primly: 'Why did you do this?'

'I thought we was supposed to kill all rats and mice because of songo fever,' the Yorkshire voice said, defensively.

'So we are. But you don't fire a rifle haphazardly in camp, even if we are in the front line. And especially in the close confines of a dug-out. You might have killed Bombardier Kingsland. Then what would you have done? Well?'

The soldier looked at him without expression, then down at his rifle.

'I just wanted to kill the blasted thing,' he said, sullenly. 'I hate them.'

'I can understand that,' said Pretty Boy. 'I don't like them any more than you do. But don't you ever do that sort of thing again. Understand? If everyone fired off his rifle just when he felt like it, can you imagine what would happen?'

The soldier didn't answer.

'And you'd better give that rifle a pull-through,' Pretty Boy added, with British Army officer verve for detail.

'What's songo fever?' I asked.

Pretty Boy looked at me and dimpled as he leaned his plumpness against the door jamb and wiped strands of damp, brown-blond hair from his round, rubicund forehead.

'Songo fever,' he said, importantly, 'is a liver disease. In many cases, fatal. It is spread by the bite of a nit that lives on the Korean rat and mouse.'

'Has anyone in the troop ever caught it?' I asked, rapidly taking off my blood-wet shirt.

'No, not yet,' replied Pretty Boy. 'Touch wood!'

'Might be a good thing, then, that we've got him around,' I commented, indicating the soldier.

Again Pretty Boy smiled and dimpled. 'But not to that extreme, Bombardier. Not to that extreme.' With that, he left.

'Stupid bastard,' mumbled the soldier.

I rolled my shirt into a ball and vigorously rubbed my chest with it. 'I take it you're Gunner Sutton?' I said.

'Stan,' he replied, taking the bolt out of his rifle in readiness for pulling it through.

21

'Kingy,' I said.

'You the new forward observation post bombardier?' asked Stan. 'The last one got a nasty attack of a bullet in the brain-box. They say an F-O-P man's life is very short. But I know I'll get through all right.'

'How do you know that?' I asked, with a calmness I didn't at all feel.

'I just know – that's all. You volunteer for F-O-P duty?'

'You *might* call it that,' I replied.

The Army liked to think, nicely, that all F-O-P men were volunteers. But I was never accorded that privilege.

On my arrival that morning at 'Easy' Troop of 4.2 mortars, I had been summoned to the dug-out of Captain Legg, the troop commander.

'I've just seen your record, which I won't remind you of,' he said. 'But your qualifications both as a TARA and signals instructor – ah, they're a different matter. How would you like to be my F-O-P bombardier? Can be a little sticky at times, but I'm sure an ex-paratrooper won't mind that. Good, then that's settled.'

I hadn't said a word!

'You can share Gunner Sutton's dug-out. He's been with me about three weeks. He'll tell you what it's all about. Oh, yes – you might just as well be my driver/operator as well. One more thing: I don't advise your wearing the Red Beret at the F-O-P – rather conspicuous – and there are quite a lot of snipers. A brown cap-comforter is much more discreet. I'm afraid we haven't been issued with steel helmets yet. Oh, yes, there is another thing – don't call me Sir when we're up there, and no rank insignia to be worn. Protection of officers should we be captured. Now I suggest you get your head down. You must be tired after the long journey.'

The instant I saw Captain Legg, a burly six-footer, I liked him. He had that quiet air of assurance that denotes someone who knows what he's doing and, like Jungle, presented to me an elder-brother figure.

When I asked Stan what he thought of Captain Legg, he said: 'Leggy's a first-class officer.' Then Stan laughed. 'The only trouble with him is he never waits for an answer!'

As I unpacked my big pack to find a clean shirt, Stan's eyes fell on the *Concise English Dictionary*.

'What's the book?' he enquired.

'My Bible,' I told him. 'Written by two famous lexicographers.'

'What's lexicographers?'

I handed him the book. 'Look it up,' I said.

'Cor!' he exclaimed. 'It's a bloody dictionary! You read this?' I nodded. 'Well, I've never heard of anyone bringing a dictionary to war!'

Changing the subject I asked him what it was like at the forward observation post.

'Sandbags, barbed wire, trenches and brown earth,' he said, 'but with a beautiful view of the Korean mountains! I've only been up there once. It was pretty quiet except for snipers and the occasional shell.'

Stan suddenly noticed something with my chest being bare. 'You're not wearing a rosary!' It was almost an accusation.

'I have an understanding with God,' I said, enigmatically. 'Besides, the only good a rosary will do you is possibly deflect a bullet or a piece of shrapnel.'

'You're a cool customer,' he said, then he asked: 'You come through Gloster Valley?'

'Yes – and noticed the American spelling on the signpost. The moment I saw the valley I thought that it was an ideal place for an ambush. It looked very sinister, even though the sun was shining.'

'The F-O-P gave its own map reference to bring your own shells on top of you in the end,' said Stan. 'They was completely overrun. All the Gloucesters and the mortar battery was wiped out. It was just like committing suicide for the F-O-P men.'

'It must take a lot of nerve to give your own map reference to the guns,' I said. 'I hope to Christ we never have to do it.'

'Me, too.'

I looked up at the ceiling of the dug-out. 'That looks pretty secure,' I observed.

'Yeah. All dug-outs are made like this out here. The command post and F-O-P as well.'

It was a simple design. A hole cut into the sloping ground, tree trunks or thick branches laid across to make a roof, then sandbags, soil and rocks piled on top.

'They keep out rain, bullets and shrapnel,' Stan continued, 'but not a direct hit. And rats love them. The roofs are ideal for nesting.'

'Yes, but no more Daniel Boone antics, OK?' I told him.

Stan grinned and started cleaning his rifle. In my clean shirt, I lay down on my camp-cot, closed my eyes and thought of Sylvia, wondering what she was doing at that very moment. Intermittently, though, I couldn't help fretting about the odds of a shell landing smack on our roof.

The first of many narrow escapes with death that Stan and I were to experience, during the year we were together, occurred the following morning. Several times I had heard the screeching proclamation of an incoming shell, giving me sufficient warning to be flat on the ground before the crump. Or I had been safe in the dug-out or command post. But this particular shell was different. There was no warning screech or whistle.

Together with a nineteen-year-old conscript called Ben Distbury, who had travelled with me to the front line, Stan and I emerged from the command post to take breakfast after a six-hour stint on watch. The blast almost knocked my eardrums out and I was hurled back against the sandbagged wall.

It was as though someone had let off a ton of dynamite, the explosion cutting off thought and befuddling the brain. Then all was still. Pieces stopped falling to earth. Dust and smoke hovered.

I found myself sitting on the ground next to Stan who was tapping the sides of his head above the ears with the heels of his palms. Ben was lying on his face and knees in a most peculiar fashion with his backside in the air, clutching his stomach with both arms. Blood poured from the sleeves of his jumper.

I sat, immobile and numb with shock and horror as the young body suddenly came to life with writhings. Ben's teeth ground themselves sickeningly together. Then came three

24

violent convulsions, choked screams, a pleading 'Fucking hell', and Ben fell over sideways, stretching his body in death. Bowels bulged through a long, deep gash in jumper, shirt and abdomen. I had never seen the insides of a human being. They looked just like a pig's or a sheep's. I noticed, besides the awful blood and shit, that Ben had kept his eyes tightly closed throughout, and now there were tears on either side of them and they were open and unseeing as the rat's had been.

I got to my feet as other soldiers and the sergeant-major arrived. A blanket was wrapped round the body and it was carried away.

Against a rock, close by, lay a piece of shrapnel. It wasn't smooth like the pieces I had seen in films at the School of Ballistics. It bristled with long, wickedly sharp needles of steel. Stooping, I picked it up – and dropped it immediately. It was still so hot it burned my hand!

I caught the sergeant-major's sympathetic and understanding eyes. 'They say you don't feel the heat,' he said, quietly. 'It sort of burns out all the nerves.'

A yell from Stan made me jump. 'Hey! Look at this, Kingy!' He was trying to dig another piece of shrapnel out of the command post's door jamb with his knife. 'This bastard bit nicked my sleeve. I'm having it as a souvenir.'

I just couldn't believe Stan's calmness and seeming unconcern over Ben's sudden death. Feeling too sick to eat breakfast I went to the dug-out and sat on my camp-cot. God! I was frightened. This wasn't manoeuvres. This was the real thing. Now where was that tough, hard-drinking Red Devil who wanted glory, I asked myself with a sneer. My thoughts went to Ben and death. What *did* it feel like to die? Because of my mother it was a question that had hounded me all my life.

As a young boy I had been forced to listen to her accounts of people dying in the village, and my infant mind had concluded that dying necessitated a definite transition from this world to the next, producing in the body a foreign, bewildering and frightening sensation that only those who experienced it would ever know – and they could never come back to describe it!

Ben now knew the answer. He was lucky. But he was going to be such a long, long time dead – and he had been so very, very young.

Only a few minutes ago we had been sitting together, talking and manning the radio sets in the command post. What would Ben have done had he known death was so close? If he had known he had seen his last sunset, eaten his last supper, smoked his last cigarette? That was a nasty word, 'last'.

I opened a packet of cigarettes and studied them, wondering if one of them would be my last. How frightened can a man possibly get, my mind screamed. God! It was awful, being a coward! Then another frightening thought gripped me – I was actually glad that Ben had been killed and I had escaped! It was a terrible – kind of superior – feeling but I couldn't help it. I reached for Sylvia's letters in an attempt to glean some comfort.

The shell which had killed Ben, so Leggy told me later, had been a morale-destroying 'loner', heralding nothing, but a necessary ingredient in a war of nerves. 'Chinky', as the enemy was called because most of them were Chinese, lobbed them over 'just for kicks' almost every day, sometimes two or three times a day. No time pattern. Nobody knew when one was coming. Some 'poor sod' often went when one arrived.

Stan and I almost 'went' again that very same afternoon. We were chopping wood for the kitchen fire, a South Korean 'Gook' picking up the cut pieces. Suddenly, there was an ear-splitting thunder-clap and the South Korean screamed and spun like a top. Then he fell, face downwards and still. There was a gaping hole where his left shoulder-blade should have been, the raw, fleshy mound around it looking like a red rose.

'That was a mortar,' observed Stan, matter-of-factly. 'Fucking good job we were behind this tree.'

'Christ!' I exclaimed, with that same frightening, superior gloating within me as I looked down on the dead South Korean. 'If this is the so-called blunt end of the Front Line, what the hell is it like at the sharp end?'

On my third day at war, late in the May of 1952, I found out. My first sighting of the enemy came at five thirty on the following morning.

For five and a half hours I had been standing, alone and miserable, in the dirt-walled and sandbagged F-O-P in front of the infantry lines and in the middle of God-forsaken desolation. I was supposed to be looking for the enemy. That was a laugh. Over and over again I had asked myself: Who the devil would venture out in this? It had been a pitch-black, filthy night – rain, wind and mud – and now it was a filthy dawn.

With first light, the black mound on my far right took on the recognisable shape of Kamaksan, a sharp-pointed, high, rock mountain. The emptiness in front of me through the observation slit gradually became the reddy-brownness of shell-ripped no-man's-land with its splintered trees and barbed wire.

I felt I was in a private Hell. England, Sylvia, Mum and Tania were a million miles away. I doubted if they even existed, such were the jumble of idiotic fears that hour upon hour of gazing into nothingness had produced. Since midnight the only assurance I'd had that I wasn't the only human left in the world was Stan's voice on the other end of the field telephone in the observation post, two hundred yards away.

My eyes had also played funny tricks, making things appear that weren't there at all. Now, I could see there was nothing out there. It was as dead as the proverbial dodo and just about as unknown, as this whole country was, to the snug, community-loving people of Buckinghamshire and Dorset.

The dark night had shrouded me with some kind of false security. Daylight brought back the stark reality of where I was – north of the 38th Parallel, right up at the sharp end. It didn't come much sharper than this. Only a narrow, empty, crater-pocked valley separated me from the enemy.

North Korea is nearly all mountains with paddy fields in many of the valleys. My first impression was that it would be a beautiful country without a war.

All forward observation posts were situated on high ground and, in the static war that then existed, the territory immediately in front was divided into sectors, code-named and drawn on a panorama board with co-ordinates inserted. On sight of the enemy, all that had to be done was pick up the telephone, give the code name, map reference, description of target and the order to fire. Every gun and mortar within range could be brought to bear on that particular target.

Because I was a TARA – a person who delved in logarithms, could use a theodolite and plot and tell where a shell should fall many miles away – the power of instant havoc and death was all mine.

It was in a trench on the other side of the valley, in a sector code-named 'Illinois', that the enemy suddenly appeared. Six of them, in single file, were trudging along the trench in the gentle rain, about three hundred yards away, rifles slung on shoulders.

I looked at them in much the same way a puppy will watch, fascinated, an animal or bird it has never seen before. Methodically, I counted them. I knew I should try to destroy them. I could shoot at least one, if not two, with my rifle. But, hell, they were human beings. Nice people just didn't go around shooting other people. I knew full well that I couldn't pull a trigger at them. That was much too personal!

My eyes went to the field telephone that could bring death to those six terrible members of the enemy, then back at them. The trench was fairly long. I could get them at the top – allowing for time of flight of shells – just before it curved round the hill. They had obviously misjudged their timing. Left it a bit late for getting back. They kept turning their heads towards our lines.

Probably shitting themselves, I thought. And, Christ, they weren't hurting anyone. Their dress at that range looked like casual sports jackets and flannels. And in this weather, too! They probably felt as dejected as I did.

Thoughts of Ben and the South Korean, lying dead, induced some incentive for me to pick up the phone. But I ignored it. I let them go.

I didn't feel proud or God-like about sparing them. I was

28

simply obeying civilised human nature not to kill. I did, however, have a smug, cowardly thought that by letting them live I had, surely, merited my own salvation!

Captain Legg didn't see it at all that way when he breezed in at five minutes to six to receive my report. In fact, he forgot his Sandhurst training to be an officer and a gentleman. He clumped me hard on top of my head with his mapboard!

'You dozy, stupid bugger!' he roared. 'Next time, kill them! D'you hear? That's what you're bloody well here for! If you don't kill them, they'll kill you! They were probably a recce party taking back valuable information. And you let them go! I've a good mind to put you on a charge!'

His voice quietened when he saw how I was feeling. 'First time you'd seen the enemy? Well, I'll overlook it this time. But we're not playing games, you know. Now, you remember what I said.'

I had cause to remember later that day when Stan and I were doing the noon-till-six watch together. We took turns, looking through the 'donkey's ears', powerful binoculars designed like a periscope so that a person could see what was going on without showing his head. Very handy, considering the enemy's abundant use of snipers. A man's head, showing through the observation slit, could easily be picked off with telescopic sights, as evidenced by my predecessor!

The mid-afternoon sun, in heat-haze blue, highlighted all the enemy hills forming the other side of the valley's boundary. Stan swung the donkey's ears back to a point he had just passed.

Excitedly, he said: 'I can see a Chink sniper!'

'Where?' I asked, equally excited.

Stan straightened from the eye-pieces. 'See that old tree? One o'clock from there, there's a small vee in the rock. He's in there.'

Through the observation slit I could see a blur of brown, and that was all. 'Let me have a look,' I said, and pushed Stan out of the way. When I put my eyes to the donkey's ears, the sniper was as large as life.

'See him?' asked Stan.

'Yes. And his rifle has telescopic sights.'

29

'Take a pot at him, Kingy. We'll never be able to direct a shell in there without giving him plenty of time to move.'

'You mean with the .303?'

'Yeah. Why not? You've got a marksman's badge. You stand a bloody good chance of hitting him.'

'No. You take the shot,' I said, like a small boy arguing with another about who should do the mischievous deed.

'No, I'm a lousy shot,' said Stan.

I took another look through the donkey's ears. The lenses were so powerful, I could see the sniper's big, brown eyes. They were set in a large, rather gentle and round face, and I remembered Jungle's words about the first man he had shot.

'You sure you want me to fire at him?' I asked, feeling a strange sensation in my anal sphincter. The thought didn't even occur to me that I could pull rank and order Stan to take the shot.

'No, you do it,' urged Stan. 'If you don't get a move on, the bugger will have gone!'

I remembered Leggy's words about kill or be killed. 'What range do you reckon he is?' I asked, trying to forget my bowels.

Stan looked at the panorama board. 'About four hundred yards,' he said.

'I'll *never* hit him at that range.' There was a hint of relief in my voice.

'Just aim into the vee,' said Stan, impatiently. 'You're bound to get him. I'll watch through the donkey's ears and tell you where the bullet went.'

I took my rifle from where it was leaning in the corner, pulled back the bolt and rammed a round up the spout. Then I flicked up the leaf sight and raised the peep-hole to the 400 mark. I pushed off the safety.

'Hurry up!' Stan growled.

I ignored him. I felt calmer now that I had the loaded rifle in my hands. Resting the Lee Enfield across the sand-bagged window ledge of the observation slit, I pointed it in the direction of the vee in the rock. Looking through the peep-hole sight, my eye automatically found the centre. I brought the front sight up until its tip was in the middle of the brown blur. The rifle was rock steady when I squeezed the trigger. The brown blur disappeared the instant the rifle butt slammed back into my shoulder.

'Yippee!' yelled Stan. 'You got the bastard! Smack in the chest! The bullet went right through him and chipped the rock behind. Bloody good shot, Kingy! Wait till we tell Leggy!'

My God, I thought, I've killed someone!

Whenever I felt afraid, for some strange reason my eyes always took on a steely light, which everyone always mistook for cold ruthlessness. Stan was no exception.

When I said, quietly and in absolute awe: 'Do you realise, Stan, I would be hanged for that in England?' he thought it was a real tough guy joke, and warmed even more towards me.

'Come on!' he said, with sublime happiness. 'Let's see if we can find another bugger!'

Thankfully, for my peace of mind, we didn't.

That night was a restless one for me as I lay in my sleeping bag in the observation post next to Stan. I couldn't get the gentle face and brown eyes out of my mind. My thoughts went to Jungle's first kill again, and I wondered if the sniper had had a photo of his wife and children in his pocket.

I reasoned with myself that the man did have a rifle, and it was fitted with a telescopic sight. But to kill him like that was tantamount to murder. *Was* murder! Then, again, snipers were doing that sort of thing all the time. That was what they were trained for. But I wasn't a sniper. It wasn't my job to do that. I had to kill the enemy in a different way.

Still, I did have to kill them. And now I had definitely forfeited any chance of salvation. No God would bother about me now, whoever or whatever He was. But I had fought and won my first battle with God when I was only five. Thinking He was always a bit airy-fairy, I had shouted to the heavens every swear-word that had earned me a carbolic-soap mouthwash. Then I'd challenged Him to strike me down dead.

With that major victory won, I had crept into the village church on the Sunday morning during Matins and fired off

31

a cap pistol. Acoustics made it sound like both barrels of a shotgun going off at once! They caught me just as I reached the lychgate. After that I was firmly convinced that all religious people were fanatics!

I wondered what Stan was dreaming about. Whatever it was, it had the accompaniment of loud snores. I was glad when the fourth member of the F-O-P party, Gunner 'Scouse' Smelley, woke Stan for the midnight watch. Scouse slept the sleep of the dead. But for a long time after midnight I lay awake.

I remembered how I always felt when shooting pigeons and rabbits on the farm. The sheer thrill of hunting for them, the eagerness to see one and pull the trigger, then the crocodile remorse afterwards.

There was one rabbit in particular I could always recall to mind. It was only a young one. I had shot it and it had crawled into some stinging nettles. Parting the nettles I found it lying with its back arched and legs kicking. The rabbit had big brown eyes, too. Its little mouth had opened and such a tiny squeak had come from it when it saw me towering above. Quickly I had snatched it up and killed it with the side of my hand, hating myself for having shot it in the first place.

I managed to derive some comfort by thinking of that rabbit for, being a typical Englishman, I felt it always better to hurt a human.

By the following afternoon, the thoughts of the night were past. The hunting spirit was back. I was on my own in the F-O-P. I knew full well, though, that if I did spot a sniper I wouldn't do anything about it. Not without Stan to give me moral support.

It was a beautiful afternoon. There was no heat haze and the enemy hills looked alarmingly near, their red-brown soil looking like newly harrowed fields. I felt I could almost reach out and knock a North Korean's head off with my rifle butt if I saw one.

Then I noticed that, with the absence of a heat haze, two hills were showing in the distance that were not marked on the panorama board. Pointing the donkey's ears at them I saw a paddy field between. More, there were white-dressed figures there.

Adjusting the fine focus I saw that they were women, working with large-spaded hoes. One of them was young and attractive, her black tresses streaming down over her shoulders from beneath a white, cloth cap.

I swept the field and saw a hut. Sitting outside it were two old men, watching the women work. They, too, were wearing the indigenous white dress of the peasant.

Picking up the phone I located Leggy at the infantry command post.

'Can you come round here? I've sighted some people working in a rice field three or four miles away.'

Leggy arrived within minutes. His shirt was sweat-soaked under the armpits and his breath stank of whisky. Binoculars swung from his neck.

'Whereabouts?' he puffed.

I told him as I was drawing the new-found territory on

the panorama board. He looked through the donkey's ears, then focused his own binoculars.

'Get the 25-pounders,' he ordered. 'They should be in range. If we don't hit them we'll probably frighten seven different kinds of turd out of them!'

'But they are *women*!' I protested.

'Kingsland,' he said, 'they are *enemy*.' He spoke slowly and with emphasis. 'They could have anything hidden in that hut.' Then his tone relaxed. 'Besides, there's nothing else to shoot at! Now be a good lad and get the guns on the phone. It will be good practice for you.'

Vague thoughts of the Geneva Convention occurred as I did as I was told, and repeated Leggy's instructions to the gunners. Leggy was using only one gun for ranging. Time of flight of the shell was thirty-seven seconds. Five seconds before the shell was due to land, the operator at the gun end gave the dutiful warning to 'Look in'. I repeated it to Leggy.

Still holding the phone, I looked through the donkey's ears. A white plume of smoke told us we were far short.

'We're in the wrong pissing gulley altogether,' Leggy snorted. 'Up seven-fifty!'

'Look in,' I said, for the second ranging shot. Five seconds went by but no smoke appeared.

'Where did that bloody thing go?' Leggy wondered aloud.

Then we saw that the women were looking to their right where smoke from the burst was rising from behind a low hill.

'Go right thirty minutes. Battery target. One round. Fire!'

This meant that all eight of the battery's guns would each fire one round.

'They are requesting target description,' I said.

Leggy hesitated. 'Oh, tell them ammunition hut. That'll keep them happy.'

I was looking through the donkey's ears when the eight shells spread themselves across the paddy field and valley.

As one, the women dropped their hoes, lifted their skirts and ran like hell. The hut and the two old men went up with a direct hit. But, so far as I could tell, all the women got away. There was not a sign of them anywhere.

34

'Cease fire,' ordered Leggy. 'Target destroyed.'

He tapped me lightly on the head with the panorama board when he saw the look of distaste on my face.

'All's fair in love and war,' he told me. 'I quite enjoyed that. Let me know if you see anything else exciting.' And he left to finish his whisky with the infantry commanding officer.

Within half an hour the women were back, picking up their hoes and bits and pieces round the demolished hut. I made no move towards the phone. A truck came up and the bodies of the two old men were loaded into it. One woman shook her fist at what to her were the enemy hills. Then the women climbed aboard and the truck drove off.

I breathed a sigh of relief when the truck disappeared. I also felt rather lonely and sad. I had quite enjoyed their distant company, brought close by the donkey's ears, especially the young, attractive one's. There was certainly no glory in shooting at them, I told myself, despondently.

Two or three weeks later, our mortar battery left the English unit it was supporting and went to another part of the front to support the 1st Australian Regiment. Forward observation posts were manned alternately by the battery's two sister troops, 'Easy' and 'Dog', the names standing for 'E' and 'D' in the phonetic alphabet used in radio transmission procedure, and it was our turn first.

'Right! Now to business!' said Leggy, producing his mapboard in the new F-O-P we had spent all night digging and establishing.

'We've heard that there's activity across there.' He pointed to a blank cliff face on the other side of the valley. 'We don't know what they're doing. Intelligence and infantry patrols haven't been able to establish that. But we do know that the little bastards are there – so watch it! And report anything immediately.' He looked hard and knowingly at me. 'No matter what it is, report it. OK?'

First light had barely appeared, and two Australian soldiers sauntered up.

'Waste of time you buggers being here,' said one. 'Nothing for you to look at. Ain't had any action here for weeks.'

'Thank you for telling us,' replied Leggy, politely.

'Watch out for the snipers, though,' said the other Australian. 'They're real bastards.'

They waved and walked casually down the trench towards no-man's-land.

'Where are they off to?' I asked.

'Those poor sods will be out there best part of the day in the sun,' said Leggy, 'sniping for snipers. I've been told they are *very* active here, so keep your heads down.'

One of the first things I found out about the Australians was that they were never short of beer! That was absolute bliss for me. The one-litre bottle of potent Australian beer served to F-O-P men each evening had fallen far short of quietening the butterflies I bred in my belly. Now, though, the generous Aussies were always handing out extra bottles!

Four afternoons later, just after six o'clock, the F-O-P seemed to explode. I hurled myself face downwards, dazed and bewildered. When I raised my head, the air inside the F-O-P was dark with dust and smoke. I reasoned that it must have been a shell. The smell of burnt explosive was strong.

God! It was so sudden! That's how I'd probably go. One minute I would be standing there – the next, I wouldn't.

Two Aussies came running along the trench. 'You all right, mate?' one asked. 'A yard higher and you'd have been a goner!'

'Did you see where it came from?' I asked, shakily.

'No, Blue. Ain't got a clue.'

The second explosion was heralded by a short, whistling scream. I instinctively ducked.

'That one was just above us,' said one of the Aussies. 'You're all right when you hear the scream, and the longer the scream, the better. You don't hear the one that kills yer.'

'Come on, mate,' said the other Aussie. 'We best be getting back to the lines. No telling what this might mean. Be seeing you, Blue.'

Violent anal twitchings and the butterflies in my belly going into a St Vitus Dance – as I jokingly called it – told me that the enemy had a 'bracket' on me. One shell below, and one above. The third was bound to get me!

I was panicking whether to obey my guts and get the hell out of there when the third shell came in. It had a much longer scream and went merrily over my head to crump in the infantry lines. Chinky wasn't after me!

I looked through the observation slit and saw a plume of smoke right in the middle of the cliff face. A plume of smoke had no business being there. Focusing the donkey's ears, I saw there was a ledge in the rock face close by the smoke and, above, a square piece that moved!

Even as I watched, the piece opened like curtains, a how-itzer shot forward, spewed a puff of smoke and recoiled back into the cliff face, the 'curtains' closing after it. The scream of the shell was as long as the last one's, the burst flashing about seventy-five yards to my right. I couldn't believe my eyes.

I was reaching for the phone when Leggy came puffing in, wanting to know what was going on. I told him, and just to prove my words, the gun popped out once more.

'Deucedly cunning, the Chinese,' said Leggy. 'That's a mountain gun. We need a tank, my lad. We'll never get a 25-pounder in there. See if you can locate the Tank Regiment.'

I pressed the switch on the remote-control unit that oper-ated our set in the infantry command post, which we were using as our observation post. Nothing happened. One of the shells must have knocked out the wires. I phoned Stan at the command post.

'The remote control is out. You start that end and I'll start this. Tell Scouse to radio the Tank Regiment. We want a tank up here fast. Description of target: mountain gun.'

'What the hell's that?' Stan wanted to know.

'I'll tell you when I see you,' I said.

I waited until another shell crunched in, then made a move. As I thought, it was the second shell that had shattered the wires, about fifty yards up from the F-O-P. Stan arrived soon after me.

'What's all the fuss about, then?' he asked.

I explained as we started to repair the wires.

'Ohhh!' was his rejoinder.

We were putting insulating tape on the repairs when a heavy-calibre machine-gun opened up at us. Stan was standing on top of the trench. I was inside, keeping my head down.

The first burst thudded in just as I was saying: 'I now have first-hand, practical knowledge why we're taught never to run the remote control and telephone wires together. You know you're in full view of Chinky up there, don't you?'

The bullets thwacked in just below Stan's feet. The force of impact sent a shock wave up his legs, he told me later, through his body and tingled his teeth. To me it felt as if a herd of elephants had landed. The vicious snaps of the machine-gun's firing had followed the bullets' crestwaves, smiting our eardrums and jarring every nerve in our bodies.

Stan looked down at his feet and said: 'Cor!'

'Down!' I yelled, and yanked him into the trench by his trouser-leg just before a second burst cut through the air where he'd been standing.

'You're bloody daft!' I said, heatedly. 'I told you about standing up there! Do you know what would have happened if one of those bloody things had hit you?'

One of the bullets had encountered a softer part of the trench's bank and its nose was peeping through on our side. I pulled it out.

'Look at the size of it!' I said. 'It's the sort they shoot at aircraft with.'

The bullet was about three-quarters of an inch in diameter and about two and a half inches long.

'That would take your arm off,' I told him.

'And your bloody head!' ventured Stan.

'Come on. Let's get out of here.'

'We ought to put some more tape on the cable.'

'Fuck it,' I said. 'It'll be all right for now. We'll do it when it's dark.'

Another shell came in as I made my way down to the F-O-P. Leggy was on the phone when I arrived.

'What was the machine-gun after?' he asked, when he'd put the phone down.

'Us,' I said, succinctly. 'And it nearly got Sutton.'

'Well, we can't get a tank here before dark. They're stationed too far away. But we'll get it into position tonight and give those bastards something to chew on for breakfast.'

Twenty minutes went by and no more shells came in.

'That'll be it for now,' said Leggy. 'They've had their fun. I'll leave you to it.'

When he'd gone I started thinking about shells. The noise they made at the receiving end was so different from the noise they made in war films. The shellburst was such a sickening, final and violently momentary thing, its blast a centrifugal force that carried shrapnel death for more than a thirty-yard radius. Not the piddling little explosions in films. Still, I reasoned, if they used the real thing, they'd kill all the actors!

I could see now just how far-fetched those big-star movies were when the hero led his men through a hail of shellbursts. Why, the blasts alone would have knocked them arse over tit!

I watched the sun go down. It was a splendid sunset, but it evoked in me a deep sense of melancholy. The earth walls of the F-O-P became cool and then cold. For the first time I noticed the smell of the earth. It was all around me. I sniffed my clothing. That, too, smelled of the Korean soil. So did my hands. And no wonder. I was living in the ground like a rabbit, and a frightened one at that. I was more than pleased when Scouse brought me my bottle of beer. It was much better company than my rifle and bandolier of fifty rounds.

I checked the telephone and remote-control box, built myself a comfortable seat of sandbags by the observation slit and began swigging. I was halfway through the bottle when I was joined by an Australian sniper, equipped with three bottles of beer!

'Evening, Blue,' he said. 'Peaceful now, ain't it?'

I nodded.

'Name's Bill,' he continued, chattily, and seated himself with his back against the earth wall. 'What's yours?'

'Kingy – short for Kingsland. First name's Gerald but I hate it. Sounds a bit lah-de-dah.'

He nodded. 'You don't look much like a Gerald. Been out here long?'

'No, just a few weeks. Seems like years.'

He grinned. 'Well, the first twelve months are the worst. This ain't a war, though. Not like it was in the desert.'

'Desert?' I asked.

'North Africa Campaign.'

'You were a Desert Rat, then?'

Again Bill nodded. 'Most of us are World War II veterans. Got tired of civvy street and bitching wives and decided to have a go again. Not like you poor buggers. You ain't even got whiskers on your chins. You've still got the nappy marks.'

There was silence while we each took a swig of beer.

'We was always on the move in the desert,' he went on. 'Here, we just sit and look at each other. Like the 1914–18 war. Bloody trenches! We just sit and snipe each other for target practice.'

Bill took out a packet of cigarettes. 'Smoke, Blue?'

'Thanks,' I said. Then: 'What's all this Blue business?'

'We calls anyone with red hair, Blue.'

'I see.' I drained my bottle. 'Seen any of the other nationalities out here?'

'All of 'em,' said Bill.

'What are they like?'

'Which ones?'

'Well, I've heard we've got Thailanders, Turks and Gurkhas.'

'Good soldiers, Blue. Bloody good. But no one can beat the English soldier. We all say that. It's because you've got the best discipline in the world. Nothing to touch it.'

'I've heard you Aussies are pretty good,' I returned the compliment.

'So we are, Blue, so we are. And d'you know why?'

I shook my head.

'Because we're too bloody scared of being cowards in front of our mates. I've seen us when we've fixed bayonets. Shit scared in our boots. Yet we've each tried to be in front of the other bloke to prove that we're braver and better than he is. But you pommies, you've got the discipline. And it was that discipline that won the British Empire. A shame to see it go.'

Seeing I had finished my bottle, Bill handed me one of his. 'Go on, take it,' he said. 'I can get plenty.'

'What are the Yanks like?' I asked.

Bill spat. 'Useless. Absolutely fucking useless. They got no discipline. They even blow themselves up in their own minefields because they forget where they've put 'em! No, the only thing they're good for is marching into a town after someone else has won it for 'em and fucking the women. The way they go about fighting, you'd think they were expendable.'

'I had two brothers in the last war,' I said, 'and they thought pretty much the same about the Yanks.'

Bill and I discussed my need to prove myself, which he sympathised with, then the conversation changed to women to finish off the beer.

Just before he left, he told me: 'If you get through this war of nerves, I reckon you can say you've proved yourself, Blue.'

'Yeah, but I've got to get through it. That's the difficult part!'

'I'll call in with a few more beers tomorrow night. They always ease the situation.'

But he didn't. To use my mother's oft-used expression when someone in the village died, God called for Bill next morning, in the form of a shell, smack on top of his dug-out. It was one of the many shells that the enemy hurled at the tank, and I had a prickle of conscience when I remembered something else my mother often told me. She firmly believed in predestination. Everything that happened in life was a pathway to another event.

When I heard about Bill I thought: If I hadn't seen the mountain gun, the tank wouldn't have been brought there and the shell wouldn't have landed on Bill's dug-out. Then I told myself not to be so stupid.

I had just settled into my sleeping bag when I heard the tank rumble into position. But I was too tired to get up and look. Just before light I was awakened by Leggy.

'I've briefed the tank commander,' he said, 'and he'll commence firing as soon as he can see the target. We'll go down to the F-O-P and relieve Sutton. Make it snappy because the tank is perched right on top of the hill, and when Chinky sees it the shit will hit the fan!'

The tank was a perfect target on the skyline, about 100 yards to the right of the F-O-P. The North Koreans started lobbing mortar shells at it long before the cliff face across the valley was clearly visible. Bigger shells started coming in just as the tank opened fire.

I watched, enthralled, as the first tank shell, red-hot and plain to the eye, streaked across the valley to blow a hole in the cliff face to the left of where the mountain gun was hidden. I focused on the smoking hole and caught movement below it. There were three North Koreans in a small observation cave watching the tank through binoculars. The shell had displaced a load of rock, uncovering their position.

'Yes, I know,' replied Leggy, when I told him.

Leggy had an FM set with him. As he pressed the switch on the microphone to speak to the tank commander, the tank's second shell hit the right-hand top corner of the camouflage curtain, and blew it to pieces to reveal a large, black hole.

'If you look just below where your first shell landed,' Leggy spoke into the microphone, 'you'll see an enemy observation post.'

He listened to the reply, then told me: 'He's seen them. He's going to pump five shells into the gun hole first.'

One after the other, in rapid succession, the tank's shells disappeared into the large cave, the first three sending back clouds of smoke, their detonations flashing and illuminating the inner walls. The flashes and smoke of the last two shells were not seen.

'They're the ones that have done the damage,' announced Leggy. 'Blown everything out the other side.'

The three enemy observers hadn't moved. The red light glowed on the FM set. Leggy put the receiver to his ear.

'Yes, I know. It's incredible, isn't it? They're still there,' he said. Then to me: 'If those Chinks have got any sense, they'll get out of there, fast.'

42

Unbelievingly, I watched the tank's shell etch its low trajectory across the valley and disappear into the small cave between the stupidly waiting observers. The inside of the cave flashed crimson. The three men came flying out as though they were being propelled on top of the smoke like table-tennis balls on top of water spouts.

They went in three different directions. One looked as though he were standing to attention, absolutely stiff; one was somersaulting in a tight ball; the third was upside down in a swallow dive. All were going upwards. There was something almost graceful about them.

They reached their zeniths, where they seemed to hover – then they were falling, faster and faster, to the valley floor, far below.

'Beautiful!' exclaimed Leggy. 'Absolutely beautiful!'

He pressed the switch. 'That was a very nice piece of shooting,' he told the tank commander. There was fervour and devout admiration in his voice. 'Come round to the command post and I'll stand you a whisky. But first, get that tin can out of sight!'

Even I had to admit it had been quite something. Well, it wasn't everyone who could say that they'd seen a human firework display! I looked up into the sky, half-expecting to see three souls soaring to heaven. Where *did* souls go to?

The souls of those three, plus the soul of the sniper I had shot, might even now be looking at me, hatefully, through the observation slit!

The thought of death was heavy with me again. The same apprehensive feeling was there but, come on, I had to admit, I had found it very entertaining.

The tank's engine started up and, ponderously, the tank backed from the ridge and out of sight.

The mortars and shells stopped coming in and the valley was peaceful once more. The sun had come up and it looked like being another beautiful day.

5

A staff jeep was waiting to whisk Leggy off to Tactical HQ for a conference when we returned to the troop after we were relieved by Dog Troop men. To my joy I found a letter from Sylvia waiting. We also found that a new sergeant-major had settled in. The previous one had finished his time and gone home.

Stan and I were soon convinced that Battery Sergeant-Major Winscombe was a bastard in every sense of the word. He soon let it be known that he held no special favours for F-O-P men. Just because we might think we were hard cases after serving at the sharp end, he had no intention of letting us interfere with his first love of Army life – bullshit.

He decided that it would be conducive to the good order and conduct of Army discipline if he did not allow the F-O-P men to indulge in the idle, cushy time they might think they had earned. So, unnecessarily, he started us digging, the day after our return, a six-man bunker in the rockiest place he could find. More, and to our disbelief, he had introduced eight-o'clock kit parades every morning!

'I wish Leggy were here,' I said to Stan, 'I'm sure he wouldn't allow kit parades. They're bloody suicidal!'

Stan and I attended the first parade, but on the second morning we decided to stay in our bedding rolls. We were pretending to be asleep when, after the parade had been dismissed, the sergeant-major marched into our dug-out. He proceeded to prod me in the ribs with his big, brass-handled stick.

'OK, you two. On your feet!' he said.

'Eh?' I murmured, opening my eyes. 'What time is it?'

Sergeant-Major Winscombe ostentatiously consulted a large-dialled watch on his thick, black-haired wrist.

'It is ho-hate-two-five hours, precisely,' he said, punctuating the words with more jabs in my ribs. The last one really hurt and ignited my red-haired temper. I jerked my body upright and made a grab for the stick. I just missed and the sergeant-major stepped back hastily.

'You do that again,' I told him, heatedly, 'and I'll take your stick and thrust it right up your arse!'

'Right! You're both on a charge! Absent off parade! Report to the command post at ho-nine hundred hours!'

'Do you, know, Stan,' I said, completely ignoring the sergeant-major, 'I can understand now why such a lot of sergeant-majors get lost in battle.'

'Are you threatening me, Bombardier?' Sergeant-Major Winscombe demanded.

'Of course not, Sergeant-Major. Just making an observation.'

The bull head looked from me to Stan and back again.

'Ho-nine hundred hours!' was all he said.

The punishment he doled out was not only diabolical, it was more suicidal than the kit parades. The Australians needed a trench to be dug for night-time sentries on the other side of the hill, facing the enemy. Stan and I had to dig it in broad daylight!

Like the proverbial coward, I began to die a thousand deaths when I saw the bare, brown hill of the enemy looking straight at me. It was so near I could almost feel it breathing down my back.

'I don't think our sergeant-major is very pleased with us,' said Stan.

I didn't answer. I began digging like a love-sick mole answering a long-awaited mating call!

Stan watched, fascinated, as I dug and tried to hide in the hole I was digging all at the same time.

'What *are* you doing?' he asked.

'I'm going down, mate. I'll dig myself in first, then I'll tunnel the trench. If you've got any bloody sense you'll do the same.'

Stan shrugged and began digging, leisurely.

'You know,' he said, reflectively, 'that hill looks awfully close. I wonder how many Chinks are watching us?'

'Probably the whole fucking North Korean Army,' I said, and increased the rate of shovelfuls per minute of the red, sand-like soil.

Just as soon as I could sit down with my head below the surface, I stopped and lit a cigarette. Stan did the same, except that he sat on the edge of the hole he had dug, with his legs inside it.

'You're a funny bugger,' I said.

'Why?'

'Aren't you scared, sitting up there?'

'No.'

'Really?'

'Really.'

'But you can be picked off by a sniper or blown to smithereens by a shell at any minute,' I protested. 'Don't you have any nerves or feelings?'

'Nope. I just know I'm going to get through this. That's all.'

'I wish to Christ I did,' I said. I looked hard at Stan. 'You really aren't scared, are you? You weren't when we were machine-gunned. God! I wish I were like you. You've either got nerves of steel or you're bovine.'

'What's bovine?'

'Thick. Oxlike.'

'Oh.'

'Why do you wear that bloody silly cross round your neck?' I demanded. 'Do you think that protects you?'

'No. But I like wearing it. Everybody wears one. Everybody was issued with one.'

'I know. It's bloody pitiful, really. They hand them out to you as though they're lucky, magical charms, then send you up here to be slaughtered. Never mind, lads, you'll definitely go to heaven if you've got one of these. Well, I refused mine. At least I had the guts to do that. Half you buggers have never been to church in your lives, except for your christenings, yet you expect to become one of

46

God's chosen as soon as you put it round your neck. What protection do you really think that's going to give you?'

'I don't wear it for protection,' said Stan. 'I just feel like wearing it.'

'Go on. You're all bloody hypocrites,' I said.

'Why are you picking on me? You religious or something?'

'I don't know what I am. Like everybody else, I automatically say I'm C of E. My grandfather was a lay preacher and I was forced to go to church twice on Sundays and once to Sunday school. Somehow, when I got older, I couldn't stomach it. Something about it all didn't ring true to me. But I'm buggered if I'm going to wear a cross now like the rest of you hypocrites just because I stand a good chance of being popped off. It really makes me gripe when I think about it. Just look at some of the rough, illiterate bastards out here. Some of them would knife their own grandmothers for tuppence. And they're all wearing crosses on silver chains like bloody convent girls!'

Stan laughed. 'True,' he said. 'Very true.'

'Like I told you, I think I've got a good understanding with God, whoever He is. And He can take me without a cross. I've never worn one before and I'm bloody sure I'm not going to wear one now just because I'm out here and scared.'

'You never look scared, you know,' said Stan. 'You look as tough as arseholes. Like digging that hole. I thought you was just making a joke of it.'

'Christ, if you only knew,' I said. 'Come on. Let's get digging.'

We had dug about five yards of trench when an Aussie infantryman came hurrying by, rifle slung over his shoulder with muzzle in hand, looking as casual as a tramp.

'That's the enemy out there,' he informed us. 'What are you trying to do?'

'We've been put on a charge for being naughty,' I explained.

'On a charge? What was the sentence? Death?' The Aussie was a real wit.

'Tell you what,' he went on, 'better loosen your bootlaces.'

'What for?' Stan asked, defiantly.

'You don't want to die with your boots on, do you? You want to be able to get them off quick!' And off he went, chortling, over the hill.

Within minutes, Leggy came snorting down to us. He sounded very angry. 'Come on, you two, get back to the other side of the hill as fast as you can!'

Safe on the other side, he went on: 'How the devil you haven't been killed, I'll never know. You were sitting ducks! Anyway, I've had strong words with the sergeant-major and you're off punishment. But you were both very naughty, you know. The Army's the Army and discipline must be maintained. And you, Bombardier Kingsland, don't you dare antagonise the sergeant-major again. He's an old soldier and he's done his share of fighting. Keep out of his way as much as possible. Understand?'

'Yes, sir,' I said. Then: 'Sir?'

'Yes?'

'Those kit parades. It seems ludicrous to me that we all have to stand out there together in the open at eight o'clock, waiting for a shell to land on us. You know that Chinky likes to lob them over for breakfast.'

'Yes, well,' he said, huffily, 'I've seen about that little matter, too. There won't be any more kit parades. But that doesn't excuse you, in any way, for what you did!'

As though on cue, the enemy lobbed in three mortars all at once at ten-past-eight the following morning, much to the discomfort of six peacefully performing gunners.

For some unknown reason, the makeshift lavatories in Korea always seemed to attract as many shells and bullets as they did flies. The Aussies' favourite reply to the question, 'Where is so-and-so?' was, invariably, 'He's gone for a shit and a sniper's got him'! Going to the lavatory could well be a very daring deed and I understood the Army expression – 'Baking it' – signifying holding back from going to the lavatory.

The latrine, or bog, was a rectangular hole in the ground with a rail across. Six lilywhite bottoms, gleaming in the sunshine, were hanging over it when the mortars came in with their sharp cracks, forming an arc fifty yards away.

There was a mad scramble to get off the rail, pull up trousers and run, all at the same time. The one on the far end was the unluckiest.

He had short legs which, when he was seated on the rail, didn't reach the ground to steady him. The bursts of the mortars made him jump so much that he fell backwards, trousers around ankles in the air. He hung upside down for a moment or two, grappling in blind panic to hold on, then he plopped into what he had just deposited and the deposits of many others!

He leapt out, caked and steaming, and began running and jumping, trying to get rid of the halter his trousers made round his legs.

Nearly the whole troop had seen what happened. Laughter, claps and cheers egged on the runners, backsides unwiped, in the handicap race to their dug-outs. The short-legged gunner, minus trousers, was last, but he got a special cheer!

That morning I realised for the first time that we were living more like animals than human beings. Going to the lavatory was no longer a private, personal act of meditation; and masturbation was no longer a shy, inhibitive topic. Inhibitions were fast falling away. Photographs – imported via Tokyo – of nude and underwear-clad models, were openly exchanged with comments like: 'I need a change. I've gone off her!' Sometimes, though, a particular photograph was possessively retained, the holder remaining 'faithful' to it for several weeks or more.

Mostly, I preferred sex-fantasising about Sylvia. But, gradually, as the weeks went by, I found the memories of her becoming more scanty than the scanties she wore in my daydreams!

One morning at the F-O-P, I said to Stan: 'Three months, now, of blood, shit, shells and rats. I suppose there is someone called Sylvia in this world? The only thing I can remember about her is the evening she undressed in a barn and walked towards me, seductively, in her high heels, stockings and suspender belt. Isn't that terrible?'

49

'I should think it's enough,' commented Stan, drily. 'But do you know what I want to do sometimes?' he mused. 'Have a hot bath and put on a nicely ironed, white shirt. There's nothing like a clean, white shirt. On Sunday afternoons, when I'd be meeting the girl, I'd have a bath and put on a clean, white shirt, then I'd admire myself in the mirror. Sometimes the shirt would tickle the end of my John Thomas. And what with thinking of the girl, I'd have a wank before going out.'

'You impetuous, polluted fool!' I told him, humorously.

We began discussing things that civilians and a peacetime Army take for granted. High on the list was a real toilet with a chain to pull! Then there were scented soap, listening to records, a mattress, sheets, pillow; a cup of tea with home-made cakes and a pint of beer in the local.

'And just imagine being somewhere where you know for sure that a shell can't come in at any minute,' said Stan. 'I can't believe that there is such a place any more.'

'Christ, yes. That would be bliss. Do you know, I've become so tense that if someone farted behind me I'd drop flat on my face!' Stan laughed. 'And I feel as if I know every crack, crevice, tree and rock in these bastard hills.'

'Yeah. Me, too. Looking at hills every day and living like we do is enough to drive anyone bonkers.'

'Funny thing, though,' I ventured, 'although we're cut off from women, there's been no report of anyone being queer or turning queer.'

'Good job, too,' said Stan. 'I don't fancy a sore arse!'

'I'm going to write a long, sexy letter to Sylvia this evening,' I said.

'OK. I'll write to my girl, too, and I can copy some of your big words.'

'You're getting as bad as the officers,' I told him. 'Now that they know I read a dictionary, they are always asking me how to spell such-and-such a word. Leggy asked me the other day how to spell crepuscular.'

'What the fucking hell's that?' asked Stan.

When I told him, he said he'd put that in his letter, too. 'If you tell me how to spell it!'

A week later, Stan and I saw our first white woman since being out there. It was the singer Carole Carr. She had come out to entertain the troops.

On the day that we went down to see the show at Tactical HQ, ten miles behind the line, the entire troop was treated to the facilities of a mobile bath unit. I took off my dirt-encrusted clothes and wallowed. It was after I was dressed in all new, clean clothes that I knew just how much of an animal I had become.

When I picked up my old clothes to deposit them in the laundry bin, the stench made me recoil. They stank of stale earth, stale sweat, urine and general fug. I was amazed that I had actually worn them and not noticed.

The Carole Carr show was open-air. When she walked on to the stage, about three hundred pairs of rampant, sex-starved eyes riveted on her. She wore a pink-flowered, silk sheath dress, high heels and tan-coloured nylons. To me she looked soft and utterly desirable. I didn't listen much to her singing. I was undressing her a dozen different ways!

We were still talking about her when we got into the back of the truck to take us back to the troop.

'The sexiest thing about her,' said Scouse, 'was the way her suspenders showed through her dress when she moved. That always excites me.'

'Me, too,' I said.

'And did you see that time when she bent over towards us?' Stan enthused. 'Wow! Those lovely white tits! I really go for tits.'

'I was sitting in front, just below the stage,' came the smug voice of Gunner Morcambe, a command post signaller, 'and when she did that high-stepping sort of marching dance I could see right up above her stocking-tops!'

That excited all of us. 'Did you see her knickers?' asked Stan.

'Yes.'

'What colour were they?'

'White, and they were silky and semi-transparent.'

'Ooohh!' we all groaned.

'Just think of a night with her!' drooled Scouse.

Stan and I certainly did that night when we got into our bedding rolls. Sylvia and his girlfriend were, literally and metaphorically, thousands of miles from our freshly excited senses.

It was only a few weeks later that another delectable young lady provided us with more material for our sexual fantasising. She also saved our lives.

Her name was Marilyn Monroe.

6

Still in support of the Australians, we had moved to a new position, west of Hill Three Five Five. I was in the command post, learning about some new sound-detection equipment when Stan came in.

'Kingy,' he said, 'there's a smashing film on at Battery HQ this evening.' Everyone had been talking about a new sex bombshell called Marilyn Monroe. The film was called *Monkey Business* and she was in it.

'I was thinking of having a beer, writing a letter to Sylvia and having a nice long kip.'

'Aw, come on!' he urged. 'There's a scene where she puts her stockings on!'

'In that case, yes,' I said. 'What time does the truck leave?'

'Eighteen-thirty hours.'

The film was everything Stan said it would be. Marilyn Monroe was absolutely fantastic. When the return truck was halfway back to the line, we saw there was a red glow in the sky.

'Some poor bastard's getting it tonight,' observed Stan.

That 'poor bastard' happened to be our battery! Easy Troop's four 4.2 mortars were blasting away for all they were worth when we arrived and the shells were coming in thick and fast. Stan and I leapt from the truck before it had come to a halt and ran for the cover of our two-man dug-out.

Only there was no dug-out. Just a gaping hole where a shell had scored a direct hit.

'My God!' I exclaimed. 'My dictionary! And Sylvia's letters!'

'We'll look for them in the morning,' yelled Stan. The noise of gunfire and shell explosions was deafening.

53

'Come on, Kingy! We can't bloody well stand here!'

We dashed to the command post and reported to Leggy that we had nowhere to sleep.

'I don't think anyone need bother about going to sleep tonight,' he told us. 'This is going to go on for quite some time. You can give us a hand here.'

'I think I'll write to Marilyn Monroe,' I said, 'and thank her for saving our lives. We'd be dead now if we hadn't gone to the pictures.'

'Oh, I should,' replied Leggy, sarcastically. 'I'm sure she'd really appreciate that.'

Next morning Stan and I found our personal effects scattered about; and there was my dictionary, together with Sylvia's letters, intact in my big pack some twenty yards from where the dug-out had been.

But that night was the beginning of battles for high ground all along the front; an offensive that was to drag on until the winter. It was later known, collectively, as the 'Battles for the Hills' stage of the Korean War. In some parts, the width of no-man's-land between the enemy's lines and those of the UN forces was no more than fifty yards! As I commented to Stan at one F-O-P: 'Why don't we just reach out and shake hands with them, or invite them over for tea?'

The one night that our battery was called on to put in a 'hit and run' attack proved to be a shamefaced disaster for me.

Before we set off – all vehicles without lights – Leggy told us, comfortingly: 'We run when the shit starts flying. There will be no time for digging-in and you will be completely in the open. But if a shell or bullet has your name on it, it will get you, in or out of a dug-out!'

Dog Troop was doing whatever F-O-P work was necessary, and to me befell the task of ammunition-truck driver. Pretty Boy was in the passenger seat, acting as quartermaster for the distribution of mortar bombs. It was an unbearably hot night and we were shirtless. Our backs looked like miniature mountain ranges with lumps from mosquito bites.

Rapidly in position behind the crest of a hill almost touching the enemy's lines, the mortars began firing. The enemy were taken completely by surprise and about ten minutes elapsed before they retaliated. Then they did so with a vengeance.

'Right! That's it!' Leggy yelled. 'Let's get out of here! Fast!'

I needed no second urging. My truck was the first away. It was like daylight with the shellbursts and I accelerated down the hill in third gear, unused mortar bombs in the back and craters appearing everywhere. My panicking mind told me that a microscope would be needed to find the bits of me if a shell landed among that lot in the back.

'Change down!' screeched Pretty Boy, as he was bounced in the air from his seat. 'You are going too fast!'

I double-declutched but couldn't get the gear lever into second. We were now hurtling down the hill. I stood on the brake pedal but nothing happened. Pretty Boy yanked up the hand brake, also to no effect. The weight in the back and the downward slope were too much for any brakes to hold. Revving the engine until it threatened valve bounce I thrust the gear lever home with brute force and a horrible noise of grating gear cogs.

A Bedford fifteen-hundredweight truck has a very low-speed, 'crawler', gear sitting right next to second. By a miraculous fluke I engaged the crawler gear. When I took my foot off the clutch, the gearbox flew apart with a loud bang. Now we were really moving! Pretty Boy was holding on like grim death.

There was a deep, wide gulley running alongside us. Edging the truck round in a wide arc so that we wouldn't overturn, I gripped the bucking steering wheel harder as we plunged down the gulley's gradual slope, taking saplings and small rocks with us. Halfway up the other side, the truck lost its momentum and, with the assistance of brakes, stopped. I then let it roll back to the bottom.

The hissing, venomous voice of Pretty Boy cut through my self-laudations on an expert piece of steering:

'You are a *cunt*, Kingsland! With you around, who needs a fucking enemy!'

I didn't mind. I was safe. The shells were falling far behind.

Pretty Boy got out and slammed the door. Then he climbed up the gulley's sloping side to thumb a lift. With irrepressible laughter, I followed.

Next afternoon, Leggy called me to his dug-out.

'Do you know what our losses were last night?' he asked, sternly. 'One pissing Bedford fifteen-hundredweight! I've just had the REME's report. The gearbox, you might be interested to know, is practically non-existent, and God knows what you've done to the differential.' Then he smiled. 'Don't worry,' he said. 'We're not going to dock it from your pay.'

Hardly a night was going by without our being called upon to engage. Both sides launched thrusts and bombardments to gain fresh ground and each battle lasted until dawn.

'Why is it always night-time?' Stan growled. 'Why can't we have a battle in daylight so that we can see what we're doing?'

Shells were ripping telephone cables to shreds and it was always the F-O-P men's responsibility to repair them.

Because of the contours at one particular F-O-P, the wires ran across no-man's-land to the command post. Stan and I always reckoned that creeping through no-man's-land on one's tod in the dead of night, trailing cables through one's hand to find the break, was enough to put anyone in a nut house! There was only a password – changed daily – between a lone repairman and death from his own side's patrols. There was nothing between him and death from the enemy.

One safety factor that was pretty reliable was the croaking of the frogs. While they were in full chorus one could be fairly certain that no one was crossing through the paddy fields.

One night I was making my way along the edge of a paddy field when the frogs suddenly stopped croaking! My neck began to prickle as I crouched, deathly still. As usual I had the rifle's hammer in the half-cocked, safety position, one round up the spout and ten in the magazine. I always liked to have that extra round for good measure.

Often I had wondered what I would do if I came face-to-face with the enemy out there all on my own. I remembered a John Wayne Western in which he threw himself flat on the ground and blazed away with his rifle without asking any questions, and I told myself, courageously, that that was what I would do.

Straining my eyes in the darkness, the prickles in the back of my neck became more intense as I discerned that it was a bad place for an ambush. There was tall grass and there were bushes all around. I began edging forward.

Suddenly, a voice hissed 'Black' right in my ear!

'Aaaarrrgh!' I cried, just like people do in cartoon strips when they get shot. My mind went a complete blank with shocking fear. 'Black' was the first part of that day's password. What the devil was the second part?

'Don't shoot! I'm English!' That was all I could think of. It would have been a scream, but I had to say it quietly. Then the second part of the password came to me.

'Dahlia,' I said, with relief.

Black-faced figures closed in, all with sten-guns pointing at me.

'It's that bloody pom!' The Australian accent was a joy to hear. 'What d'yer think you're doing out here, Blue?'

I told them, adding: 'You almost frightened me to death.'

'Well, don't hang about here too long. There's a Chink patrol in the vicinity. And be a bit quicker with the password next time.'

The figures disappeared and I was alone again. I carried on tracing the cables and found the break a few yards further on. As far as the darkness and my none-too-steady hands allowed me, I made the repair, connected a telephone and, thankfully, received a reply from both ends. Attaching the telephone and repair kit to my belt, I picked up my rifle and made a bee-line for the F-O-P.

The vicious smacks of sten-gun bullets jarring into the hill above me made my heart jump with fright. Then a small-arms battle broke out in the paddy field below. The enemy patrol had been encountered. There were two lines of gun flashes, one nearer to me than the other. My fear-filled mind was

57

still able to tell me that the bullets which had nearly cut me in half had come from sten-guns. That meant that the enemy was between the Australians and me! Just to leave no doubt about it, another burst of sten fire almost took my head off.

Sod being killed by my side, I thought, frantically, and I ran with all my might to the left. Squatting down, I listened. The two patrols were still hard at it, but no bullets were coming my way. Bent almost double I ran up the hill, turned right, found the communication trench and staggered into the F-O-P.

Stan was sitting there, swigging beer from a bottle.

'Been having fun down there?' he asked.

I said nothing but took the bottle from him and put it to my very dry lips.

7

Lack of sleep was becoming a serious problem. Stan and I were reaching a point where tiredness outweighed danger. In one set of four days we'd had five hours' sleep. I was ready to throw in the towel. On the fourth morning I got into my bedding roll at three o'clock only to be awakened by Stan at four.

'Chinky's started again,' he told me, laconically.

'I don't care a monkey's toss,' I replied, angrily. 'The bastards can come and kill the lot of us. I just want to sleep. Tell them we'll join them.'

'Don't be daft,' Stan insisted, and kept on shaking me violently until I just had to get up or have my eyeballs jerked from their sockets.

Then, thankfully, next day the North Koreans must have become just as tired as we were, for the frequency of attacks and battles began to lessen.

Sergeant-Major Winscombe took the opportunity of the lull to organise sleeping rosters in the afternoon, together with swimming parties to the River Imjin which flowed near to that part of the front.

On my first trip I thought I had arrived at Brighton beach. Every company and battery out there seemed to have had the same idea of an afternoon bathe to freshen up before the likely skirmish that night. The only difference was the absence of bathing costumes and women.

The Imjin was wider than the London part of the River Thames, its fast current keeping to the centre, leaving its shallow edges almost pool-like with their borders of golden sand.

These shallows and lath-like beaches on the northern side now bristled and bustled with naked bodies of every hue under the sun.

One of the first things that caught our attention was a coloured US soldier, standing knee-deep in the water and lathering his body with soap. Stan and I had heard stories about black men, and now we were witnessing it. To say that this soldier was well-endowed would be an understatement.

'I feel definitely inferior,' I told Stan, with awe in my voice.

'Yeah. Me, too. I bet he's excused PT shorts.'

We undressed, covered our comparatively small private parts with our hands like bashful maidens and walked quickly out into the water until our inferiority complexes were covered. I could have sworn I saw the soldier grinning at us, derisively.

Contemplating the distance to the far bank I asked Stan if he was a good swimmer.

'Pretty good,' he responded. 'Why?'

'How about having a go across to the other side?'

'I don't know,' said Stan, doubtfully. 'It's pretty wide.'

'Come on,' I urged. 'Let's have a go.'

We fixed our eyes on a tree on the other side and began swimming steadily towards it. The water grew colder and we began to feel the mild tug of the outside current. The tree had moved away to our left. Then the current was strong. The tree vanished upstream and we were being swept sideways round a wide bend in the river.

'Keep plodding towards the bank!' I yelled. 'Just take it easy.'

It was a funny sensation, swimming forwards but going sideways instead. A frightening sensation was when the racing current swept us downwards a few feet before throwing us up to the surface.

I thought about Sylvia and remembered how proud of me she had been one hot summer's day when Pug and I swam the two and a half miles across Weymouth Bay. I wondered what she would think of this swim and it occurred to me how perspectives changed according to circumstance. Weymouth Bay had been quite a challenge but I would have been far too frightened to have done anything like this, which would have seemed too dangerous and stupid.

Yet out here, where there was constantly the chance of being blown to bits or stopping a bullet, this swim was relegated on the danger scales simply to good, daring sport. 'A piece of cake', in the words of the wartime RAF.

The current lessened and soon we were in the shallows. We dropped our feet and thankfully waded ashore, where we spread our naked bodies full-length on to the hot sand.

'Whew! That was really some swim,' said Stan, proudly.

I nodded. 'Trouble is, though, we've got to get back.'

'Christ!' exclaimed Stan. 'So we have. Sod you and your ideas, Kingy.'

'We must be nearly à mile downstream,' I said. 'What we'll have to do is walk back along the bank until we're the same distance upstream from where the others are. Then we should land right by them.'

Our bodies quickly warmed by the sun and sand, we set off at a fast marching pace along the bank. We rounded the bend in the river and there on the other side was our sergeant-major.

Like an old mother hen looking for two lost chicks he was strutting along with four other members of the troop – all of them stark naked – searching for us. When he saw us he shouted and jerked his arm in a beckoning movement for us to come back immediately.

'I don't think our sergeant-major is very happy,' opined Stan.

I cupped my hands round my mouth and shouted that we were going right upstream to start the swim back, then Stan and I started jogging along the bank. When we finally dragged ourselves from the river after the long swim back we found that Stan had been quite right about our sergeant-major. He wasn't at all happy.

'I'm putting you both on punishment when we get back,' he stormed.

'What the hell for?' I demanded.

'Deliberately endangering your lives while on Active Service,' he said.

'Balls!' I exploded.

'We'll see about that when we get back, Bombardier.'

Sergeant-Major Winscombe took us straight to see Leggy on our return to the troop.

'Yes, Sergeant-Major,' said Leggy, surprisingly, 'I know just the job for them. Tomorrow morning they can start nice and early collecting all the unexploded mortar bombs, making a neat little heap and blowing them up. I'm sure they'd love to do that.'

'The bastard!' said Stan, when we were in our dug-out. 'Fancy him siding with the sergeant-major.'

'I suppose he had to, really,' I explained. 'After all, Leggy did countermand his orders last time, and it wouldn't have been good for discipline if he'd done it a second time.'

'But we weren't deliberately endangering our lives, as he put it,' persisted Stan.

'I expect we could have drowned,' I replied. 'That current was pretty fierce.'

'Yes, I suppose so,' said Stan, grudgingly. 'I must admit that once or twice I didn't think we were going to make it.'

'Ah, well,' I said, 'at least we can always boast that we've swum the Imjin.'

'And twice, at that,' rejoined Stan.

Next morning a very chirpy sergeant-major woke us at six o'clock. Luckily, the battle during the night had been a short one, lasting little more than an hour. Even so, I was reluctant to leave my bedding roll quite so early. But I did with hardly any grumbling because this punishment had Leggy's sanction, and Stan and I began our chore.

The battery had experienced a spate of 'bad' ammunition – mortar bombs which failed to fire because the propellant housed between the bomb's tail fins was defective.

A double safety device in the nose of the bomb stops the firing pin from being driven home and exploding the bomb before time. One is a screw cap over the pin itself – which is removed before dropping the bomb down the barrel – and the other is a ball-bearing locking device which is dislodged from its locking position by the movement of the bomb in flight.

During the past couple of weeks there had been three types of misfire: complete misfire when nothing happened;

quarter misfire, sending the bomb a little way up the barrel, when it would fall back with a nerve-jarring clunk; and half misfire when the bomb was lobbed out to fall a few yards away, causing everyone to throw themselves flat.

All the 'duds' were carefully placed in small heaps a safe distance from the mortars.

To Stan and me those heaps looked very ominous and death-dealing.

'Right! Get on with it!' commanded a gloating sergeant-major, pointing with his stick. 'You can explode them in that far gulley over there. Let me know when you need the dynamite and fuse wire.'

It seemed to Stan and me that he walked away from us just a little bit more hastily than usual. I put out a hand and touched the hard, cold shell of a bomb. I could quite easily be looking at hard, cold death. But lately I had reached an understanding of sorts about death. Could it be I was getting used to its constant proximity?

'Come on,' I said, with forced humour, to Stan. 'You can only die once, I suppose.'

'I know,' he replied, 'but I've grown accustomed to the idea of dying quietly at an old age. Getting blown to bits doesn't appeal to me one scrap.'

Gingerly, we each picked up two bombs by the tail fins, one in each hand, and began walking, rigid like children carrying cups of tea upstairs to their mothers, to the gulley about 250 yards away. Any other members of the troop who were about gave us decidedly wide berths.

Stan and I were sweating by the time we carefully laid down the first four bombs. They had become much heavier after the first 150 yards and our hands were aching. We sat down and each smoked a cigarette right down to a tiny dog-end before going back for another lot.

During the morning four shells came in, one exploding just short of the gulley.

'Cor!' said Stan. 'A little bit further and it would have saved us the trouble.'

My guts would have screwed up even tighter if they'd been able to. Constantly on my mind was the thought of what might easily have happened to the safety ball-bearings and other parts inside the bombs. After all, the bombs took a nasty knock when dropped down a mortar barrel – anything could have been jolted slightly out of place. Perhaps it only needed a further small movement to make any one of them go off.

And on top of that, having to walk by that new crater was doubling the tension and agony. With each journey I became more numb and insensitive to the fear that was screaming inside me. I was like an automaton in a trance until the final journey, just before midday, when my mind came awake to scream that one of the last bombs would certainly get us, or an enemy shell would land on the heap just as we got there.

But nothing happened, and we reported to the sergeant-major to collect the dynamite and fuse.

'Don't forget, Bombardier,' said Sergeant-Major Winscombe, 'walk away after lighting the fuse. Don't run. You have sufficient time.'

It was quite a sizable heap we had to blow up.

'My God,' said Stan, 'it's going to make one hell of a bang.'

We pushed the box of dynamite through a tunnelway we had left to the centre of the heap, connected the fuse and played out the several yards of it.

'Ready?' I asked.

Stan nodded. I struck a match and put it to the end of the fuse. The flame spluttered along it at an alarming rate.

'Let's go!' I said. We began walking quickly, each of us visualising the fast speed of the flame up the fuse and calculating how far we would get before it reached the dynamite.

As one, our minds screamed: 'Not bloody far enough!' And we broke into a run. Even so, we were only half the distance to the troop when the bombs went up. Stan was right. It was a hell of a bang. The ground shook under our feet and we threw ourselves flat. Dirt and small stones splattered all around and on top of us.

'That cunt of a sergeant-major,' said Stan, with feeling. 'Now I'm really sure the bastard doesn't like us.'

'I know,' I said. 'It's a bloody good job we didn't walk.'

The blast had been felt in the command post and a huge black cloud of smoke hung in the air, blocking out the sun.

'That will give Chinky something to think about,' I mused.

'He'll probably think the whole troop has blown itself up,' said Stan.

The following night, the troop almost did. We engaged with the enemy at eleven o'clock. Shells were crunching in and the four 4.2 mortars were firing rapid. Suddenly there was an explosion which sounded somehow different from all the rest. Sergeant-Major Winscombe came running into the command post.

'Number Two gun has blown up,' he told Captain Legg. 'It's rather nasty, I'm afraid.'

'Right,' said Leggy. 'You come, too, Bombardier.'

Outside, it was ear-splitting. In the flashes Number Two gun looked like a peeled banana. Its thick, steel barrel was split down its sides and curled back almost to its base. A mortar bomb had exploded inside it.

Sergeant David Hinton and his four gunners were in a terrible bloody mess. That he and two gunners had been killed instantly was obvious. The other two were moaning. Sergeant-Major Winscombe gave them morphine injections and the medical corporal wrapped blankets around them.

'Sergeant-Major,' said Leggy, shouting to make himself heard, 'get this gun-pit cleaned up as soon as possible and organise a new gun and crew. You, Bombardier, get back to the command post and radio for a helicopter. We'll get these two out of here as soon as possible.'

Within a few minutes of my radio call an ambulance helicopter came in, illuminated by the flashes and sending dust swirling everywhere. The two wounded were strapped securely on to its two outside stretchers and it was up and away in a trice.

'It's a terrible thing about Sergeant Hinton,' said Leggy, when we were inside the command post. 'Absolutely terrible.'

'I know,' I replied.

Not only had Sergeant Hinton been a married man with

two small daughters, but he had finished his time and was due to go home the very next morning for demob.

Getting killed on his very last night out there brought home to everyone the despairing thought that you could be killed right up to the last minute. You weren't safe until you actually got on the boat. Why, you could even be killed in Seoul, with the bombing raids that were going on there.

'I reckon he ought to have been sent down to HQ this afternoon,' I said.

'I did suggest that to him,' replied Leggy, 'but he said he wanted to stay. He was a damn good soldier. I've got a very tricky letter to write to his widow. I'll organise a collection for her. And I'll make damn sure there's a full enquiry into that particular batch of ammunition. There's some talk of sabotage in Seoul.'

God, I thought, what a rotten, stinking, lousy war this is. And what a rotten, stinking, lousy country. What the hell are we doing out here, fighting for it? And fighting for what? It isn't worth it. Why don't we let the slit-eyed bastards fight it out for themselves? And what good was it being a damn good soldier? It wouldn't help Mrs Hinton and her daughters.

Sylvia was certainly right about war being hateful. My thoughts went to her and the time when I would be going home. But, my God, what a hopeless, desolate gulf of death I had to go through before that time came. Every day would be a fifty-fifty chance of making it. How on earth was I ever going to exist? There was no escape. No escape at all. Unless, of course, I could get a small wound! I looked at my hands. Would it be worth losing one, for instance? The left one, maybe, but not the right one.

The next day was really oppressive, with black thunder clouds about. I was out alone, looking for a break in the telephone line which connected the command post to Battery HQ. About three-quarters of a mile from the command post the cable followed a dirt road across a valley in full view of the enemy. Bending low and with the cable in one hand I sped across the road and found the break on the other side of the valley where the road went through a small rock gap.

After mending the cable I sat down and smoked a cigarette. Then I connected the phone and received a reply from both ends. Stan was on the command post telephone and I told him I was coming in.

Just as I was about to set off, the enemy began shelling the road.

The shells were really making a mess of the road and the telephone wire, but the awful, terrifying thing was they were fired at random intervals. One shell would come in, quickly followed by another. A short gap, then four came in. A five-second wait, then a shell on its own. And so on. And they were coming in first one end of the road, then the middle, then my end.

Suddenly there was a short scream and a shell burst and echoed in the gap above me. I was trapped! The road on the other side of the gap wound round even closer to the enemy hills. They had seen me. I couldn't stay where I was. I just had to run the gauntlet of the valley road. Besides, the word 'DUTY' screamed at me in capital letters. My duty was with the troop and my immediate duty was to maintain connection between the troop and Battery HQ.

But the last detonation had dazed my mind and I saw blood trickling down my fingers. Something – shrapnel or splintered rock – had seared the back of my hand. Desolation, loneliness and self-pity engulfed me. I thought of Sylvia, Mum and Tania and that I was now going to die and, truly, never see them again. More, there was absolutely nothing or no one to help me. I had to face this alone.

I began to cry. The sobs shook my body as I cowered against the rock wall. I flinched with the detonations as three more shells crashed on to the road midway between me and the other side of the valley.

The sobs subsided and I felt drained of emotion. I called myself all the filthy names I could think of: You stupid, cowardly bastard. What are you? A sniffling wretch who can be as brave as hell when there is no danger. Oh, you're so brave when you're drinking and fucking all those women! But look at you now! Coward! Your father's probably looking at you right now and is disgusted with you.

I started to run, my mind visualising over and over again the blinding flash, the pain and then the empty nothingness as a shell hit me. I was nearly halfway across when I heard two long screams and the thunderous double detonations. I threw myself full-length even as my flustered and fear-crazy mind tried to tell me they were long screams. Long screams, you fool! I looked back and there were two clouds of smoke hanging in the gap where I'd been cowering.

Jabbering like an idiot, I scrambled to my feet and ran all the harder. Then, joyously, I was safe on the other side. My lungs were gasping because they just couldn't get enough air inside them – but I was safe. When two more shells flashed, sickeningly, on the road where I had been lying I felt an elated, victorious sense of having outwitted the enemy. I was really proud of myself. I had done it. I had been afraid, totally afraid, but I had done it. Surely, that was real bravery.

I sat down behind the huge rock that was sheltering me from the enemy and lit a cigarette. Then I began thinking about heroes and cowards. I came to the conclusion that it all depended on moods. If you felt happy-go-lucky and your bowels were working smoothly, and the circumstances were right, you could, quite probably, become a hero.

But, as Jungle had said, you'd be a hero only in the accepted sense of the word: big, bold, fearless. The image of paratroopers and SAS men, for example. The hairy arses. The supermen. But there was absolutely nothing superhuman about jumping out of aeroplanes.

No, there was more to being a hero than simply being a bold, fearless man. Alcohol, of course, was an admirable asset when entering for the medal stakes. I had heard of several 'heroes' who had charged machine-gun nests single-handed, throwing empty beer bottles at the enemy. Come to think of it, I'd never heard of anyone throwing *full* beer bottles!

There were other ways you could become a hero; by being too bloody scared to know what you were doing, like I was most of the time; or having a nice, kind Sir recommend you for decoration. The lowest decoration was a Mention in Despatches. Probably I'd get an MID, I thought with a smile – a Mention in Disgust! After several more reflections I decided that medals should be done away with. The cowards of one day were often the heroes of the next – and vice versa.

I thought how lucky women were. They didn't have to worry about being heroes or cowards. It would be nice to be a woman. At least I wouldn't be out here. Of course, I could be the next best thing: a queer. No one would expect a queer to fight. I quickly rejected that thought. It was revolting!

The good cry had done something for me. Shells were still tearing the road to bits. I looked round the rock at the bursts, then at the enemy hills. And for the first time my look was of hatred and defiance. I was determined now about one thing – I was definitely not going to die for those Chinky bastards and their pox-ridden country. Like Stan, I was convinced that I would get through all this, get back to beautiful England and marry Sylvia.

All those silly bastards who had died were dead and there was nothing anyone could do about it. Well, good luck to them, wherever they were now – but 22274600 Bombardier Kingsland wasn't going to join them for many a year; not if he could bloody well help it!

Another shell crashed in. God above knew what the North Koreans were shelling the road for – probably target practice. Again I looked from the burst to the enemy hills and stood up, facing them.

'Arseholes!' I yelled at the top of my voice. 'Fuck the bloody lot of you!'

Then I tapped in the phone, gave Stan my position and told him to bring a reel of cable and bandage and lint for my hand.

'We'll have to re-route the line completely,' I said. 'Chinky's playing silly buggers with it.'

Two nights later I saw someone else cry. I had taken a truck down to HQ to get ammunition. A young Irish soldier, who looked barely eighteen, had come in with the last draft to Korea and was waiting, nervously, to join Dog Troop.

'Will you take him back with you, Bombardier?' asked the staff sergeant. 'You can drop him off at the troop. It will save us a journey.'

We threw the young soldier's kit into the back of the truck with the ammunition, then he sat up front with me. He hardly spoke as we drove along in the moonlight. I noticed how he kept unbuttoning and buttoning his tunic pocket.

Soon we could hear the bursts of enemy shells. Dog Troop was being hammered. I increased speed to make a run for it but the road was receiving most of the shells. I looked across at the young Irishman. His face was illuminated by the bursts, and tears were streaming silently down his cheeks.

'Don't worry,' I told him, with compassion, 'it's not half as bad as it bloody well looks and sounds. You'll make out all right.'

Seeing the boy cry recalled to me my first day out there and the nightmarish thoughts that had been with me. Now, I realised what a changed man I was; impervious to other men's deaths, cold-minded and confident – a veteran of the line. With what I had seen and survived I felt strangely superior to the young Irishman. And with that tough superiority I found I could impart a gentleness to a fellow in need.

8

Just west of the Samichon River lies a small range of hills known collectively as The Hook, because of their shape. There the blood ran freely for nearly seven months in some of the most vicious battles the war ever saw.

To the 7th United States Marines, The Hook was a combination of Guadalcanal, Okinawa and Iwojima. The Marines always boasted that they never gave ground. They did, though, when the North Koreans charged them in a seething, screeching, suicidal mass. Even worse, nearly all the enemy's attacks were heralded and maintained by tuneless blasts of bugles.

But the Marines had a reputation to uphold. Within hours of withdrawing and licking their wounds they were ready to go in again, supported by one of the biggest artillery barrages of the Korean War. We went in with them. And that was my introduction not only to the blood-spattered Hook but to fighting at close quarters.

As the Marines massed in a long line along the valley road to the rear of The Hook, I drove the F-O-P party in the jeep to a forward position. It was an October evening, chilly and overcast. It was my first look at this saga-sung fighting unit, the pride of America's Forces. Christ, I thought, even the majority of these are little more than youngsters.

The Marines looked cold, exhausted and utterly vulnerable. Some smoked, shakily but hard, as if to glean every possible ounce of comfort and satisfaction out of the cigarette. To some, as everybody knew, it was going to be that bloody evil last cigarette.

Others were busy writing letters home – last letters in many cases – the writing paper propped on their knees. I

71

couldn't help thinking that here, in living flesh and blood, was real cannon fodder.

Our battery of mortars was brought up close. We quickly established our F-O-P on a hill by the side of The Hook. Under Leggy's direction, the Royal Artillery opened up. The Marines' own F-O-P officers were also directing shellfire, and the US Airforce came in with a vengeance. The Hook became a mass of explosions and smoke. Then the Marines went in.

'Right-ho, me lads,' said Leggy, heartily. 'Let's go!'

And off we went to join the Marines.

How we got up there in one piece is difficult to say. The North Koreans didn't like leaving The Hook and they were throwing every type of shell imaginable at it. The air was alive with hisses and swishes and we found ourselves instinctively ducking our heads, and holding on as the jeep danced and bucked in and out of craters.

All night the shelling continued. In fact it didn't let up for nearly two days. All anyone could do was sit it out. It is said that the human body can become inured to almost anything, and I found that my body and ears became accustomed to the thunderous percussions and vibrations that shot through me almost every minute.

On the second night, Scouse was killed instantly as he was running along the communication trench to the F-O-P. A mortar bomb fell virtually on top of him. His remains were taken away by Marine medics.

Even the imperturbable Stan was shaken. And I threw my new-found determination of 'coming through it alive' straight out of the window. I never bothered about going to the lavatory, and when I wanted a pee I just aimed it through the dug-out entrance.

As Stan commented: 'Even your cock isn't safe out there!'

On the third night, the North Koreans put in a full-scale attack to reclaim The Hook. A Marine, who introduced himself as 'Alabama – that's where I'm from, boy', joined Leggy and me in the F-O-P just as the bugles began blasting and the bullets came whamming in.

'It's gonna be a son-of-a-bitch tonight,' said Alabama.

Leggy looked at me, raised his eyebrows significantly, and smiled.

I didn't like the bullets one little bit. Unlike shells, they had a low trajectory and could come in through the entrance and observation slit. But we were to experience a more terrible and frightening weapon, far more morale-destroying than bullets and shells.

We saw a red flash from across the valley, and the flash streaked towards us, then over our heads to explode with a crash that shook the F-O-P. Then we heard the sound of its coming.

'My Christ!' exclaimed Leggy. 'They've got rockets! Where the bloody hell did they get *them* from?'

'Russia,' I said, matter-of-factly.

It was no secret that the Russians were sponsoring the North Koreans. While we had been supporting the Australians an enemy patrol had been shot down in no-man's-land. The Aussies found that the leader was not only wearing the uniform of a Russian officer but was a Russian woman!

'Serve the fucking bitch right,' was the Aussies' comment.

Reaching for the phone, Leggy asked me: 'Can you make out where that bastard came from?'

Into the phone, he said: 'Get the tanks on Channel Dog and stand by for relay if necessary.'

'I think it was Omaha,' I said. 'It was too far right for Paris – and there's more of them now, to the right and left of the first one.'

Leggy put a finger into his ear. 'Good,' he said, down the phone. 'Relay that we've now got rockets giving us the works from Omaha. Tell him to bring as many of his bloody tanks as he can round to the left side and to check with us if he needs us to help him to range on target.'

To me he said: 'In the meantime we'll put the mortars on to them. This will be a last-minute softening up before they really charge. Make it a Battery Target.'

As I picked up the remote-control microphone and pressed the switch, the chilling blasts of bugles increased.

'The bastards will be coming any minute now,' said

Alabama, and he eased off the safety catch of his carbine.

'Fox Two to Fox One. Over,' I said.

'Fox One. Over,' came a bright response through a load of crackling atmospherics.

'Fox Two. Battery Target. Rockets. Omaha. Troop salvo ranging. Fire. Over.'

'Fox One. Battery Target. Rockets. Omaha. Troop salvo ranging. Fire. Over,' the earphones replied. Then: 'Time flight twenty-eight seconds.'

I began counting. 'Look in,' I cried. And there were the four bursts just short but in line with the flashing rockets. I pressed the switch.

'Fox Two. Up one hundred. Battery Target. Five rounds. Fire. Over.' Again the orders were repeated by Fox One.

The bursts from the eight mortars dotted themselves among the rocket flashes. As the fifth round of eight mortars landed, there came the unmistakable and comforting cracks from four tanks to the left.

'They didn't waste much time getting into position,' commented Leggy. The telephone he was still holding made a noise. He put his finger into his ear again. 'Oh, he did, did he?' he said, after hearing the message. 'Well, tell him I'll stand him another whisky when this is over.' He put down the phone.

'The old bastard. He said he didn't need our help to shoot straight.'

'I hope he's right,' I said.

The rockets were really hammering us now. Dirt and shrapnel stabbed the air and sprayed the earth wall behind. It was like facing a cock-eyed firing squad using tracer bullets. With the distension of distance every rocket appeared to be coming straight at us when it left the launcher. Then, thankfully, it would veer to the left or right or go over us.

'One thing,' said Alabama, voicing my very thoughts, 'if we get a direct hit we won't feel a thing.'

A thunderous crash hit us. The blast knocked all three of us flat and brought piles of dirt and torn sandbags on top of us.

'That was very close,' I said.

'I should learn to keep my big mouth shut,' said Alabama, blowing dust off his carbine.

Still more bugles began to blast and a Babel of shouts, screams and rifle-fire added itself to the din. In a dug-out adjoining the F-O-P two Marines manned a machine-gun that now joined in the crescendo.

Many a soldier has said it. It has also been yelled out by many distinguished actors, especially in Western films. Alabama yelled it now: 'Here they come!' And he began firing.

Leggy wiped the dirt from the remote-control box. He pressed one switch. No light. He pressed the second. Still no light. When he pressed the third, the red bulb glowed, warmly.

'Fox One to Fox One. Over,' he said, calmly, calling the control station. After the acknowledgment, he continued: 'Fox One. Monkey Target. Monkey Target. Monkey Target . . .' It was the codeword for every available gun and mortar to fire. 'Fire the bloody lot till I tell you to stop,' he added, unnecessarily but with a show of spirit, after he had given the directions.

Then all hell let loose. The whole valley and surrounding hills glowed. The screams and bursts of our own shells were as deafening as the enemy's. Those bloody bugles were still sounding. In the valley it was carnage. Figures were running. Figures were falling. Figures were being hurled bodily into the air. Figures were disappearing in licks of flame.

I stood at Alabama's side emptying magazine after magazine. I never bothered with aiming. I just fired in the general direction. There were hundreds of them out there – like ants. I was bound to hit one. I told myself, idiotically and resignedly: If everything suddenly goes black, I'll know I'm dead.

Still the rockets were coming. But only from two places now. The advancing mass had reached the foot of the hill.

Leggy pressed the switch again. 'Monkey Target. All drop two hundred,' he ordered. This would bring our own barrage very close. The shells would skim us.

I suddenly realised I hadn't heard the machine-gun for a while. I went to look. The two Marines were very dead. One was missing above his shoulders.

'They've had it on the machine-gun,' I shouted to Leggy.

'I'll go,' said Alabama, and left. The machine-gun started up again.

Leggy's lowered elevation brought our shells so low over our heads that we thought they were enemy shells coming in. With the first volley a sheet of flame spread itself along the foot of the hill.

Leggy pressed the switch. 'Bloody good firing,' he said. 'Just keep 'em there – and fast!' Leggy never bothered much with radio transmission procedure, especially in moments of emotion.

'We must be killing hundreds at a time, now,' he told me, cheerfully.

The gunners were really going it. The wall of flame hardly died. Any North Koreans who got through were systematically slaughtered by small-arms fire.

'There's a bastard coming up our trench!' Leggy shouted, and fired his .38 revolver at him. Several Marines who had also glimpsed the North Korean fired at the same time. He disappeared backwards.

'Got him!' Leggy yelled, gleefully, and blew smoke from the barrel.

The thought came to me that Leggy and his revolver were like a small boy and his cap pistol. It was a silly thought at a time like this but I couldn't help recalling how Leggy would practise on birds or on the metal direction signs the Royal Engineers had erected on the earthen roads to the various HQ bases. He would suddenly draw and empty his revolver at them as I drove him in the jeep.

But now he was firing at the real thing. He blazed away with enthusiasm.

'Oh, if mother could only see me now!' he cried.

The machine-gun stopped and Alabama stuck his head in. 'There seems to be some massing to the right!' he yelled.

Leggy quickly ordered the 25-pounders only: 'Go right fifty minutes.'

I shouted as I saw six North Koreans coming up our trench. Leggy jumped to my side, his .38 roaring. The North Koreans cowered. Then two 25-pounder shells ploughed into them. We watched as three of the North Koreans took off in high backward dives and fell from view. The other three just disintegrated in the twin flashes.

'Beautiful!' gushed Leggy, and pressed the switch to tell the guns so. But nothing happened. The third and last remote control was dead.

'Fuck! And double fuck!' said Leggy. It was an expression he always reserved for times of stress. He picked up the phone. There was no answer.

'Can you get along there and see what's happened?' he asked me. 'Oh, and watch out for yourself.' Then he turned back to the observation slit, his .38 at the ready.

I made sure my magazine was full and made a dash for the observation post. In between the ear-splitting detonations I heard the raucous whispers of bullets. The ground was shaking under my feet as I ran. A burst of machine-gun bullets screamed as they ricocheted from the top of the trench, showering and stinging the left side of my face with dirt. I paused, panting, and wiped my face with my sleeve. Sweat instantly turned the dirt to mud. I was scared to the point of numbness. Too scared to feel afraid. A shell exploded less than ten yards away, its blast flattening me into the trench and kicking rock and dirt down upon me. I picked myself up and ran on, my ears ringing and the noise now muffled by whatever had happened to my eardrums.

The observation post was full of dirt when I got there. Stan had just finished digging out the wireless set. Seeing my dirt-caked face, he quipped: 'What do you think you are? A fucking Commando?'

'Where are the reserve sets?' I asked him.

He showed me. A huge slab of rock was sitting on them.

'Where's Jock?' I further asked.

'He left ages ago. He took all the dead batteries for recharging.' He pointed to where another slab of rock was sitting on the battery charger.

'My God!' I exclaimed. 'I hope he makes it all right.'

'He's tough enough,' commented Stan.

Jock McCleod was our maintenance sergeant. A soft-voiced, Highland Scot, he was broad-shouldered, ram-rod backed and he had a prominent nose. He always called us 'Sassenachs' and we, in turn, said he was a 'heathen savage' whose father, no doubt, still swung a claymore!

Stan and I put our only wireless set back on the trestle table.

'Let's hope the pissing thing still works,' I said. 'Connect it up while I test the phones.'

A wire was off the F-O-P phone. I reconnected it and turned the generator handle. Leggy answered almost immediately.

'The observation post has had a direct hit,' I told him, 'but Sutton's OK and McCleod has gone for more batteries.' Then I briefly explained about the sets. 'I'll test the guns' phone now,' I added. 'Yes, that one's OK,' I said a few moments later.

'Good,' replied Leggy. 'Things are really hotting up in the valley. They are throwing all they've got into it now. Tell one troop of mortars to go right twenty-five minutes, then see if you can get the new nine-inch howitzers on the phone. I'll give you the range later.'

'Right,' I said, and gave the mortars their fresh orders.

'All the aerials have gone,' Stan announced.

'What, all bloody four?'

'Yep. But the set seems to be working all right.'

'Make one out of cable. I've got to see if I can get the howitzers.'

Stan quickly worked out the aerial formula for the frequency and studied the hole in the corner of the roof that the shell had torn.

'I'll put the aerial out through there,' he said.

I went through the exchanges at Regimental and Tactical Headquarters and got the nine-inch guns on a weak line.

'I've got the howitzers,' I told Leggy.

'Relay Battery Target. Zero Two Zero Degrees. Elevation Nine Thousand Five Hundred. Right Section Ranging. Fire. Request Time of Flight.'

I repeated the orders to the guns and received the acknow-ledgment. Stan came panting back into the command post from fixing his makeshift aerial.

'Christ!' he said. 'You could get killed out there!'

He got busy with the set. Within a minute he was speaking to Control. 'Tell Leggy to press the remote,' he said. The rotary transformers whirled to transmission.

'Thank Christ that third section is still OK,' I said.

'Can you come back here and give me a hand, now?' Leggy asked.

I handed the two phones to Stan. 'If I don't come back, make it roses,' I told him.

'You mean bloody dandelions, don't you?' he replied with a grin.

I looked up at the hole in the roof. 'You should be all right,' I said. 'They say that shells never hit the same place twice.'

'Let's hope the bloody shells know it,' was his retort.

I put my head down and went like the wind. Leggy was giving more orders to the howitzers when I reached the F-O-P.

'They're charging the wire,' he said, handing me the remote-control microphone. 'Tell all mortars to drop fifty.'

As soon as I'd put down the microphone, I pumped off ten rounds rapid.

The North Koreans were making suicidal dashes to the barbed wire. I saw one dive madly into it just as a mortar bomb got there. The man's innards suddenly flowed out in front of him like firemen's hoses. He clutched himself, then Alabama's machine-gun made sure he left his misery behind.

Leggy was blazing away again with his .38. He had ranged the howitzers on to the wire and they were waiting his order to fire. Leggy was also waiting – for that final surge.

The odd bullet or two was still smacking the F-O-P but the rockets had almost ceased. My rifle was getting very hot. And still the North Koreans kept up their suicidal dashes in ones and twos and in small groups. Leggy turned his head to grin at me. Then he crouched and reloaded.

'Won't be long, now,' he said.

Several times he ordered individual troops of guns to fire elsewhere. Bodies, some mangled, some limbless, were beginning to pile up on the wire.

The bugles suddenly rang out above the screams and gunfire. Then hundreds of North Koreans were running to the wire.

Leggy picked up the phone. 'Fire!' he ordered. Stan relayed the command to the howitzers.

The North Koreans were mostly in a struggling, screeching heap, treading on their dead to get over the wire, and the leaders were across when the eight nine-inch shells came in with one mighty crump. An earth tremor shot through the F-O-P and through to the other side of The Hook. Every Marine felt it.

The shouting and screeching suddenly stopped. The moon went behind a cloud but the white smoke could still be seen, rolling back from where the barbed wire had stretched.

The moon came out from behind the cloud and, through the straggling plumes of smoke, we could see the devastation. There was hardly any wire left. The eight shells had dropped with deadly accuracy.

The ground looked as if a farmer had been spreading manure. But the heaps were crumpled bodies.

The smoke rolled back further, over the heads of the North Koreans that had survived and who had stopped in shock and horror. Then, in one group they were running away, the machine-guns and rifles cutting into them.

'What a bloody useless, senseless waste of lives,' I said, bitterly, and meant every word of it.

But the Regular Army man within Captain Legg had no time for sentiment. He quickly ordered a creeping barrage at fifty-yard intervals to slaughter them as they ran.

'The more bastards we kill now, the less there'll be another time,' he said, contentedly.

The firing gradually died down and finally stopped. A frog in the paddy fields ventured a croak. His friends and relations took heart and gave voice, too. They would carry on talking until dawn or more gunfire.

I looked up at the sky. It was all so quiet and peaceful,

it could be a romantic summer's night, with just the frogs' chorus. A natural noise on a natural country walk.

There was nothing there at all that indicated danger. Yet all those men were lying dead. The holocaust that had killed them had gone off into the night. It was no longer tangible and I couldn't perceive it, either.

I felt like saying to all those heaps of bodies: 'It's all right, you can get up now. There's nothing in the air to destroy you.'

My thoughts went to the Buckinghamshire village of Whitchurch and the remote farm on which I was born. I saw the little bridge over the stream where I used to catch minnows and sticklebacks, and run barefoot among the buttercups, and my feet would turn yellow with the pollen. To me, it was all very difficult to believe. They must be there still, but they were so very, very far away.

Then Leggy was speaking. 'I'm going to have a scout around to see what the situation is.'

Alabama came into the F-O-P. He wiped his sleeve across his forehead.

'Whew! What a night!' he said. 'My whole hands are tingling and shaking. Do you think they'll come again?'

'No,' said Leggy. 'I think they've had enough for tonight. But we'll have to keep a sharp look-out. I'll get some beer sent down to you.'

9

After Leggy had gone, Alabama crouched and lit two Chesterfield cigarettes, the flame of the match cupped by both hands, and handed one to me.

'He's a pretty cool feller,' he complimented Leggy.

'He never flaps,' I replied. 'That's the best thing about him. But he gets scared just like the rest of us.'

'You seen him scared?' asked Alabama, with surprise.

'Well, either that or he was sensible. We were filling sandbags one afternoon. We really needed a few more for a forward observation post. We'd filled the bags we had with us but there were a few more in a niche further up the slope from where we were and in full view of Chinky. We started walking up and I was using the shovel as a walking stick. We had got about ten yards when a sniper's bullet punched a hole through the shovel's handle, about an inch below my hand.'

'Christ, man, that must have really shook you. What'd you do?'

'Jumped down pretty quick. Leggy, that's what we call him, looked up to where the sandbags were and then at me. "Feel like getting a medal?" he asked. I told him I didn't. "No, neither do I," he said. "The bloody sandbags can stay there till it's dark." But another time he would have gone up there and said, "Sod 'em". Only two or three nights before someone suddenly screamed that there was a North Korean tank coming up the valley — '

'A tank!' Alabama interrupted me. 'But the Chinks haven't got any tanks!'

'I know, but this bloke said he had definitely seen one. "I'll have a look," said Leggy. And he picked up a bazooka and dashed up the valley on his own.'

'Jeez, he must have guts to have done that,' Alabama asserted.

'Yes – that's what I mean,' I went on. 'I'm sure that everybody gets scared at some time or other, no matter how tough he acts and looks. I remember one night when the shells were coming down like rain. Five of us were huddled in a small dug-out when a sub-lieutenant we call "Pretty Boy" came dashing in, asking for two volunteers to mend the telephone line. And not one of us moved! I think we were all on the verge of shell-shock.'

'Yeah,' sympathised Alabama, 'I know the feeling. What happened?'

'The bastard delegated the responsibility to me. "Detail two men to mend the line, Bombardier," he said, and ran like hell to the command post. Shit! I must be more of a moral coward than a coward. I didn't have the guts to detail anyone to go out in that shellfire. I said to my oppo, Stan, "Coming, Stan?" and we both went out and fixed the line.'

Alabama smiled, his teeth flashing white in the black stubble of unshavenness. 'I don't think you're any kinda coward,' he said, quietly.

'But I'm scared nearly all the time,' I countered. 'I was bloody scared tonight, I can tell you.'

'Scared, man?' exclaimed Alabama. 'I positively had the screaming shits. Shells and bullets I can stand, but not those rockets! After that experience tonight, I could certainly do with some R-and-R leave again. Rest and Recuperation I really need.'

'That's a bloody good idea,' I retorted. 'I haven't been yet.'

'Then you haven't lived, man. You haven't lived. Those Japanese dolls are a wow. How long you been out here?'

'Over five months,' I told him.

'Then you're eligible, man. You're eligible. I'll see the leave lootenant tomorrow – today, I suppose. A leave party's going off next week. He'll get you on it.'

'Thanks, but I'll have to ask Leggy's permission first. What's Tokyo like?'

'A dream, man. A dream. You can buy the dolls for twenty-four hours at a time. If you buy one at, say, three

83

o'clock in the afternoon, she's yours until three o'clock the next day. They bath you first, too, man. Get into the bath with you. They like to have you nice and clean. And if you buy one for three days, you get a discount! It's really big business there, man. But I didn't go in for this discount business. I bought a different one every twelve hours. I like to sample them all, man!'

'Alabama, you sound like a dirty bastard,' I said, and he laughed.

'That's for sure,' he said.

I laughed, too, but for a different thought that crossed my mind.

'It's funny how the brain works,' I said. 'When we were facing those rockets, I kept thinking that I would now prove my father's prophecy about my death to be wrong.'

'How's that?' asked Alabama.

'He always said I would hang!'

'What?' exclaimed Alabama, laughing again. 'You're kidding! Were you some kinda criminal or something?'

'My mother always said I was the son of Satan, and I *was* pretty evil when I was a boy.'

'Whadya do? Kill somebody?'

'Almost,' I replied. 'I was always getting beatings for something or other, and one day my father was coming for me with a stick and I had a loaded four-ten shotgun in my hands. I was only eight, but shotguns were part of farm life. I fired my first twelve-bore – you call it twelve-gauge – when I was six. I let him get within ten yards and I pulled back the hammer. He stopped dead and I put the gun up to my shoulder. "Take another step and I'll kill you," I said, but I was frightened out of my wits.'

'Did he keep coming?'

Before I could answer, two Marine medics put their heads inside the F-O-P and asked if there were any casualties. They took away the two dead Marines who had manned the machine-gun.

'Go on,' prompted Alabama.

'The rest is a bit hazy,' I said. 'My mother started screaming from the doorway of our bungalow not to shoot and for

Dad to come back at once. He turned and walked to the bungalow. I eased forward the hammer, laid the gun on the grass and fled to the fields. I didn't return until nightfall, thinking it would be forgotten. But, no – I got a thrashing from both my mother and my father. The thing is, to this day I can't be sure if I would have pulled that trigger or not had he kept on coming. I often discussed it with Mum when I was older without being any the wiser. But deep inside I think I would have pulled that trigger. Like I said, I was pretty evil.'

'What other things did you get up to?' asked Alabama.

'Oh, lots of things. When I was five, to prove my undying love for a village girl I promised to marry, I hanged the cat. It was almost dead when Mum arrived! Then there was Mum's pet robin. I blew it to bits with a shotgun. It had its back to me and I thought it was a sparrow! Not that that excused a beating. One late afternoon, I accidentally set fire to a new haystack in the village churchyard. I remember being clutched firmly by my father and the village policeman, absolutely terrified, and watching the red-faced and sweating firemen trying to save the near-by hedge. "I will let you deal with him, sir," said the policeman, and my father did, with a stick.'

I was telling Alabama about firing the cap pistol in church when Stan arrived with the beer. And we sat, talking, drinking and cat-napping until dawn.

When the sun came up, five US planes came zooming in. Just across from The Hook was a small mound, known to be a labyrinth of tunnels and dug-outs. It was a good jumping-off point for a North Korean attack. It was once taken by UN troops but found to be too hot for habitation.

The leading plane, carrying 500-pound HE bombs, circled high above the hill while the other four carried on and banked in straight-line formation. They came roaring in at low level with the sun behind them, and released their terrible loads of napalm bombs. All of us on The Hook instinctively ducked as the first stick hit. But nothing happened.

It was the same with the second, third and fourth planes.

The bombs littered themselves with dull thuds all over the mound, but there was no explosion or flame.

'They're just dropping the petrol bombs without the incendiaries!' exclaimed Alabama.

The four planes joined their leader, then he made off and banked.

The mound was by now saturated by the bursts of the highly volatile napalm bombs. The vapour from them danced in the sunlight. Flak appeared with sharp cracks and hung in the sky like round balls of cloud all around the planes.

'Jeez, it's gonna be a big bang, man,' said Alabama, as the leader came hurtling in.

But the plane wasn't coming in with the sun like the other four. It was higher and in line with us! We saw the HEs leave the plane's wings and silently arc towards us like black stones.

'The bloody fool's overshot!' I yelled.

All but the last two bombs suddenly dipped and exploded into the mound. There was a terrific whoosh of flame and the mound looked like a gigantic torch.

The last two bombs sailed on towards us. One landed in the paddy field, the other smacked in at the foot of The Hook. The F-O-P blurred with the shock wave. Earth and rock rained down for several seconds.

'Jeez,' said Alabama, 'I thought I was a goner.'

'Fucking stupid Yanks!' I yelled. 'Why didn't the bloody fool come in like the rest of them?'

Ignoring the insult, Alabama just shrugged. 'I guess he wanted to be spectacular,' he said.

The plane in question was doing a victory roll above us. Then, with the others on its tail, it headed off in the direction of Seoul.

'I guess I wouldn't have liked to have been on that hill,' commented Alabama.

'No,' I replied. 'I bet there's nothing alive there now.'

But I was wrong. We watched, amazed, as first one head then another appeared after the flames and black smoke had gone.

'They must be dug in right down to Australia,' said Stan, forgetting our geographical situation.

Above: A mortar observer watches both for targets and for incoming shells like the one that blasted the author on his first morning at the front.

Below: A view from a sandbagged emplacement, showing the vulnerable road which stretches towards The Hook, one of the most heavily contested series of hills.

Above: 'Dig yourself in first, then tunnel the trench,' was the author's technique for staying alive when 'probably the whole North Korean army are watching from the near-by hill'.

Below: Taking a wash is no longer a private occupation! The Third Battalion Royal Australian Regiment enjoy a 'home made' mobile shower.

Twenty-five pounders — the guns Leggy used to frighten the women working in the rice field — move forward through the snow.

Above: The enemy practised intimidation with loud speakers against these relaxed Black Watch soldiers.

Below: A forward observer watches for targets in the snow. At one point the temperature was down to fifty-seven degrees of frost.

Above: The 'Mad Mile' was a road enclosed by camouflage netting and constantly under enemy surveillance. The author often drove it, going like the clappers to beat the mortar explosions.

Below: Hill Three Five Five under attack. The author was one of four British soldiers on the hill whose orders were to stay and direct shellfire even if they were the only ones left.

Above: The bar at the Inchon rest home for Commonwealth troops: fortunately the perimeter fence had a convenient escape hole for libertines.

Below: A few men from the Duke of Wellington's Regiment have a drink at The Supporting Arms, the pub on the front. The author described these young conscripts as 'more lambs to the slaughter'.

Above: After the Duke's came the Fusiliers, here setting up a mortar. 'Regiments come and regiments go,' said Stan, 'but we go on for ever'. The author spent thirteen months at the front.

Below: South Korean porters bring provisions over the hills to the front.

Two of the most important aspects of life on the front: cleaning guns...

...and writing letters home. The author's final letter to Sylvia was possibly his most descriptive of all. It contained only Korean earth.

More realistically, Alabama was silently taking aim at a head. The carbine spat. The head disappeared.

Within an hour, the North Koreans started shelling us again. It was sporadic but very harassing. In the afternoon I asked Leggy about R-and-R.

'Yes,' he said, 'I think we could all do with that. How long have you been in the front line?' I told him. 'You can consider yourself a veteran now, especially after last night. I'll arrange it so that you can go on leave when our turn's finished up here. Let's see, that'll be in seven days' time. Not too long to wait. Just make sure you keep your head down until then. Sutton can go with the second batch. I think I'll go then as well. I'll have to see about a replacement for Gunner Smelley first.'

That evening, as Alabama and I were drinking beer in the F-O-P, Victor Sylvester dance music came wafting across the valley. The North Koreans were up to their usual tricks with loudspeakers to show that their morale was very high, and to get on our nerves, for the same record was played over and over again.

'Don't they have any more records?' exclaimed Alabama. 'It's the only one I've ever heard them play!'

Infuriatingly, we now and then found ourselves beating time to the music. Stan waltzed in with more beer, bowed low and asked, sweetly: 'Would you care to dance?'

'I know what I'm going to do,' I said, and picked up the telephone. 'Battery Target. Paris. Five rounds. Fire. Target description: Victor Sylvester. Over.'

Pretty Boy, in the command post, decided to play along and sent over the forty mortar bombs. The music continued but the mortar bursts were enormously good for our morale. We waited for the usual propaganda message to be interspersed in the music, but it didn't come.

Instead, a priest and several North Koreans, followed by 'meat wagons' – as ambulances were called – emerged from across the valley and began cleaning up no-man's-land.

The Marines took the opportunity to collect the rest of their dead – the ones who had to be dug out of the instant graves in which shells had buried them. Some had been there for more than four days; since before the Marines were driven off The Hook.

In the morning, Stan and I were requested to go to the rear side of the hill to help load the bodies quickly while Leggy and Jock kept watch in the F-O-P.

An identification label had been tied to an ankle of each body. It was estimated there were two hundred bodies. They looked like two thousand to me. The loading of them was anything but ceremonious. They were heaved into the backs of ten-ton trucks like carcases of beef. Two hundred bodies took quite a time to load and shells were still coming in. Speed was more essential than ceremony. 'Get rid of the dead and let the living go on fighting,' was the general attitude.

'You can earn a lot of money doing this at meat markets,' grunted Stan as we lifted a bull of a Marine.

'I know,' I puffed. 'I reckon we ought to put a bill in to the Marines. And by the way, why is it I've always got the shoulder end?'

'Because you're a nice, kind, strong bombardier who thinks only of his men.'

We asked about Scouse when we couldn't find him and were told that his body had already been taken away by a UN truck.

About midday when the autumn sun was at its highest, five US planes carried out another napalm raid on the mound across the valley. More flak than usual greeted them and the bursts were nearer to the planes.

As the fourth one came screaming in, a black ball of smoke shot from it. The plane seemed to stand still but its engine flew on to disappear behind a far mountain. A small black shape that could only have been the pilot, hurtled behind it, then dropped short. The main body of the plane also plunged straight to earth, leaving one wing to oscillate down like a penny thrown into water.

Then the leading plane came in and dropped its HE bombs. Load gone, and the pilot went into the usual victory roll. A shell burst just beneath him and smoke streamed from the engine. He came out of the roll and banked, losing height fast. Seconds later he went out on his 'chute and floated down just on the edge of no-man's-land.

'I think he's gone into that valley by Nevada,' said Leggy. The plane had carried on to crash behind Battery HQ. 'We'll take the jeep and see if we can bring him in before the Chinks decide to get him.'

With me at the wheel and two Marines in the back we hurtled down the hill and across to where we'd seen the airman drop. There was no sign of him.

'Stop here,' ordered Leggy. 'We'll walk up that low ridge for a better view.'

But there was still no trace of the airman or his 'chute.

'He's lying low,' said one of the Marines. 'He probably thinks he's landed in Chinky land.'

'I think you're right,' agreed Leggy. 'We'll spread out; but keep your heads down. That hill over there belongs to Chinky.'

We spread out, bent low, and began calling softly to the airman. Suddenly, a shot rang out, narrowly missing a Marine on my left. We ran to where the shot came from, and there was the pilot, wild with fear, crouching between two rocks. One arm hung useless, the fingers and sleeve caked with blood. The shoulder was ripped and bleeding.

To me he looked like the starling I shot with my first air rifle when I was five. It had looked up at me just like this all those years ago, one wing spread out, broken at the shoulder and dragging on the ground.

Like that starling, the airman looked pitiful and defenceless now that his means of flight had been destroyed. And like that starling's open beak, the pistol in the pilot's hand seemed small and insignificant. As we approached, the airman brought the pistol up to his head.

'Don't!' screeched a Marine. 'We're Marines!'

The pistol was slowly lowered as the words rang true to him and he realised he was safe. His body shook and he began to cry. Then he pitched forward on to his face.

Gently, the two Marines picked him up and carried him to the jeep, where they cradled him in the back. Two mortars crunched in, close, as I started the engine.

'Let's get to hell out of here!' yelled Leggy.

For the last three evenings before Dog Troop was due to relieve us, Alabama joined me quite a bit in the F-O-P. He was a cheerful, happy-go-lucky Regular Marine with a very rich Southern drawl. He loved to croon songs of the Deep South and I loved to listen. The songs were mostly romantic and I would often forget where I was or that shells were continually crashing outside.

On the last evening I ventured to Alabama all the things I'd heard about GIs. To my surprise he nodded.

'They're the dogoes, man. The dogoes. That's what we in the Marines call the ordinary American GI. Why, we won't even walk on the same side of the street. If we see one approaching, we cross over to the other side. They're trash, man. Trash.'

'Well, one thing,' I said, 'you Marines are certainly different.'

'We're the best, man. The best,' Alabama replied, modestly.

I didn't argue. 'There's a song we sing about you lot,' I continued. 'It's not very complimentary. Instead of "From the Halls of Montezuma" we sing "From the Whores of Montezuma".'

Alabama hummed the tune of the Marines' Battle Hymn as I sang the words. He was highly amused.

'That's pretty good, man. Pretty good. Hey! Is that what you guys really think of us?'

I shrugged. 'I think it's probably because you boast such a lot,' I said.

'But we're the greatest, man. The greatest. And every Marine is proud to be a Marine.'

'There you are,' I said. 'That's what I mean. You're always boasting.'

'We don't boast, man. We just tell the truth. We're big. We have our own ships, our own planes, our own transport. Our own everything. We're just great.'

I gave up. In any case, so far as I was concerned, the Marines were pretty good. I had no cause to complain. I changed the subject.

'I'm sorry you couldn't get on the leave party. I'd have liked you to have shown me Tokyo and the best places to go.'

'You'll have no trouble finding them,' he assured me, with a laugh. 'There's only one bad thing about R-and-R. Do you know what that is?' I shook my head. 'Coming back out here!'

'What do you think of this war?' I asked.

'We're not paid to think. We're just paid to fight. I'll say this much, though: I was at Iwojima and Okinawa, and this is worse.'

'Yes,' I said, 'but imagine dying in this poxy hole after going through such famous battles as those. It must be terrible to die here after all that.'

'One place's the same as any other for dying,' was Alabama's comment.

'Ah, well,' I rejoined, 'with luck I'll be well on my way to Tokyo this time tomorrow.'

10

'It would be just my luck if I got killed now,' I said, to no one in particular.

With a motley bunch of UN soldiers I was being shaken about in the back of a ten-ton leave truck as it tore along an earthen, Royal Engineers-made road through paddy fields. The North Koreans had chosen that moment to send in a few badly aimed shells. I shook my fist at the enemy hills.

'Bastards!' I roared. 'I wants me oats!'

It raised a few chuckles from the English-speaking soldiers. A shell ripped the road about fifty yards in front of us. The driver of the open-backed truck tried to brake but he was going too fast. The wheels hit the newly formed crater and daylight appeared between all of us and our seats, bringing curses in four or five different languages. The driver put his foot down again, hard, on the accelerator.

'Christ!' exclaimed a New Zealander, sitting next to me. 'That bastard's going to get there before his accident!'

The truck screeched round a bend, out of the paddy field and into the mountains. It was a beautiful morning, and the danger zone soon fell far behind the speeding truck.

By the time it reached the M-S-R (Main Supply Route) I was singing our battery's 'anthem':

> Hear the blowing of bugles,
> Hear the patter of feet,
> One-Twenty Battery's in full retreat,
> Oh, we're moving on,
> We'll soon be gone,
> We'll be travelling far
> Down the M-S-R,
> Cos we're moving on.

Several others joined in the second verse:

> The Chinks are a-coming up Three, Five, Five,
> The Yanks are pulling out down the other side,
> Oh, they're moving on,
> They'll soon be gone,
> They won't stop to boast
> Till they get to the coast,
> Cos they're moving on.

The truck sped on towards Seoul, the singing and laughter wafting to the South Koreans working in the paddy fields along the route.

The New Zealander, known as 'Kiwi' – like the rest of his countrymen – had been on R-and-R before. We took a liking to each other. About my age, he was fresh-complexioned and had black, curly hair. When we were almost at Seoul, he said: 'We'd better decide where we're going to meet up in Tokyo, just in case we get separated.'

'What's the name of the camp we go to in Tokyo?' I asked.

'Ebisu. But I think it will be better if we meet outside somewhere. I know! I'll see you in the bar of the Tokyo Rose Garden between o-one hundred and o-one hundred-thirty hours after we've been deloused.'

'OK. How do I get there?'

'Just ask any cab-driver. He'll know.'

We reached the Seoul transit camp with more than four hours to spare. Kiwi was right about our being separated. His flight would go at 6.30 p.m. and mine thirty minutes later.

'The first thing I'm going to do here,' I told him, 'is have a good crap in a real lavatory.'

Kiwi laughed. 'Wait until you see it!' he said. 'It's an experience never to be forgotten. Come on, I'll show you.'

The lavatory was as packed as an East London pub on a Saturday night. It was just a huge wooden hut with a rusty corrugated iron roof, bulging at the door with every nationality in the UN forces.

Kiwi slapped me on the back. 'Good luck, pal,' he said. 'Watch your arse.'

I nodded, took a deep breath and began fighting my way through the heaving shoulders to what, in a pub, would be the bar. I finally broke through and stopped short. I had never seen anything like it.

A long, bench-like seat, with holes about a foot apart, ran the full length of the wall in front. There were no dividing partitions. About twenty men were sitting on it, their trousers at different positions between ankles and knees. The stench was overpowering.

Hardly had a backside been lifted than another was plonked down in its place, the poor chap who was leaving barely having time to pull up his trousers. Everyone had to wipe himself sitting down. If he'd stood up, he'd have been bustled out before he could do so.

'Christ!' I said to myself.

Seeing that a soldier immediately in front of me was preparing to leave, I dashed in quickly to find myself seated between a stubbly-bearded Thailander and a burly French-Canadian. There was less elbow room than there is at a formal banqueting table. I looked up and met the steady gaze of a Turk and the desperately imploring look of a coloured US soldier.

I managed a grin, then closed my eyes, pretending I was on my own.

The four-prop Globemaster transporter began its descent on Tokyo at about 11.30 p.m. I felt the pressure on my ears, held my nose and blew. The noise of the engines came back with a roar.

'Boy! Get a load of that down there!' someone exclaimed.

I looked through the small window as the plane circled. It was breathtakingly beautiful. I doubted if any city, not even London or Paris, could look so colourful from the sky at night.

Millions of lights, all the colours of the rainbow – that was my first look at this impressive Oriental capital. I remembered reading how Arthur Helliwell described it in the *People*: 'Put a roof over Tokyo and you have the biggest

94

brothel in the world.' The lights of Tokyo were certainly a roof: a brilliant carapace.

In a small part of my mind, though, I wished that Sylvia were with me. But excitement and desire for sex flattened that train of thought almost to oblivion. Besides, I told myself, with what I'd been through I deserved what I hoped to find down there.

'All those generous girls down there,' said another soldier, 'just waiting for us!'

I smiled. I looked harder at the lights and wondered just where, at that very moment, was the first girl I would go to bed with.

'There's me, right up here,' I mused. 'We've never met. We don't even know that we are going to meet. And yet in six hours' time I'll be in bed with her.'

I was picturing her in my mind as the plane landed. Then we were in trucks heading for Camp Ebisu.

A young Irish soldier came into the camp's bath house, waving a piece of paper.

'Hoi've never been so hoomillyated in hall me blessed loife!' he cried. 'Me mudher would be speechless if she could see this. It says: "T'is is to certify that 22584315 Gunner O'Malley, J, has been *decontaminated*." Did you ever hear the bloody loikes of hit?'

'Get stuffed, Paddy,' another soldier told him, good humouredly. 'We saw your underpants walk away on their own when you took them off!'

We were all stripped naked and our clothes dumped in a large bin in the 'delousing chamber', as it was called. Then we were made to run the gauntlet of DDT sprays.

As we walked in file down the centre of the room with arms raised, several medics stood on either side with spray guns and squirted our armpits and heads. Two medics waited at the far end with spray guns in their hands and evil looks on their faces. The first gave us a blast between the legs from the front, and the second blasted us up the rear.

After that it was hot showers, the all-important chitty of decontamination and a sweet-smelling, fresh, clean uniform.

With 50,000 yen (about £38) and a five-day pass in my

pocket, and excitement tingling inside me, I set my new blue beret, walked out through the gates and hailed a taxi.

After nearly six months of living in earthen trenches and burrows like a scared rabbit, I felt overwhelmed. It was the first and only time in my life that I experienced 'culture shock'. I expected a shell to come screaming in at any minute or to hear the staccato crack of a rifle. But there were no shells or bullets in Tokyo – only taxi-drivers!

I'd thought I was a fast driver, but Tokyo taxi-drivers seemed to have attended a kamikaze school. I arrived at the Tokyo Rose Garden at a quarter-past one in the morning very much in need of a drink. I couldn't believe that my driver – who obviously had a licence to kill – had actually got through some of the gaps in the swerving traffic. Brushing door handles at high speed and racing starts from the traffic lights were purely routine occurrences.

After one almost head-on collision with another taxi, I had tapped my driver on the shoulder. 'Listen, mate,' I told him, 'I've had enough of danger. Take it easy.'

'Me know! Me know!' he replied, nodding his head, vigorously. And he went even faster! I decided to say nothing more.

The Tokyo Rose Garden was ablaze with lights and crowded. I eventually found Kiwi in one of the bars, talking to a beautiful Japanese girl who looked as plush as the exclusive restaurant.

'Hi!' Kiwi greeted me. 'Meet Nikki.'

I nodded. The tall, slim girl was swathed in a white, ankle-length dress with a blue, tight-fitting waistband, geisha-style. She flashed her teeth at me in that smile peculiar to her race.

'Well,' Kiwi went on, 'how's it feel to be civilised again?'

'I haven't got used to it yet,' I replied. 'And the bloody taxi-driver nearly killed me.'

'I know,' said Kiwi, chuckling. 'Frightening, aren't they?'

Glancing significantly at the girl, I said: 'You don't seem to have wasted much time.'

'All we're doing here is eat,' Kiwi replied. 'The trouble with Japanese dolls is that they haven't got much tit. And that's what we are going to find tonight: some tit.'

'We won't find it here, then?' I asked, looking at the girl's bust, flattened by the garment. 'I like legs better than tits.'

'Then we'll make a good team,' said Kiwi, happily, 'because I doubt if we'll be lucky enough to find two with big tits. What do you want to drink?'

'A John Collins,' I said.

As Kiwi was ordering, another girl, almost a replica, joined us and linked her arm through mine.

'Make that two John Collins,' Kiwi told the barman.

'The girls here are just hostesses,' Kiwi explained to me. 'Look, buy them drinks, but don't touch. Not unless you've got about thirty thousand yen to throw away. No, I've got a nice little hotel lined up where we can get it for two thousand five hundred yen. But first we are going to eat here in style. And I'm having fish eyeballs and rice.'

We downed another John Collins each, then went through to the restaurant. The two hostesses were very disappointed when we didn't invite them.

I followed Kiwi and ordered fish eyeballs and rice. After the initial shock of seeing eyes looking up at me from the plate, I found myself enjoying the special flavour. The excellent wine that Kiwi asked for helped considerably in washing the eyeballs down.

Kiwi called for another helping of eyeballs but I decided to forgo the second helping and drank a glass of saki. When we left the Rose Garden at half-past two in the morning, Kiwi was feeling 'just a little bit sick'.

We walked to the small hotel and found we were the only ones in the bar. We ordered more John Collins.

'You want girl?' asked the barman.

'What else? What else?' exclaimed Kiwi. 'Whadyerthink we're here for?'

A bowing manager was promptly fetched. He promised us two of the most beautiful girls in Tokyo.

'Yeah, well, bring 'em in and we'll give 'em the once over,' said Kiwi.

When the manager had gone, Kiwi told me: 'The first two will be awful; so will the next two, but perhaps the third pair will be all right. You just leave it to me.'

We sat sipping our drinks. Suddenly, the door was slid open and two giggling, golden-toothed girls were ushered in. They were ugly!

'Christ, man!' Kiwi yelled at the manager. 'What is this? Get them out of here! Whadyerthink we are? Desperate?'

The smiles on the two girls' faces never faltered. They left the bar and we went back to our drinks. The next two girls were as coarse-faced as the first.

'Come on,' Kiwi told the manager, heatedly, 'you can do better than that. We want tits!'

But the third pair looked just as bad, and Kiwi said so. The manager became agitated.

'These two very beautiful,' he babbled.

'Balls!' shouted Kiwi. 'Come on, Kingy, let's go!'

The manager wrung his hands.

'Wait! Wait!' he pleaded. 'Me find you two princesses. Me promise. But will take maybe twenty minutes. They come from other side Tokyo.'

'Yeah, OK,' said Kiwi, winking at me, smugly, 'we'll wait.'

The manager bowed and left hurriedly. The minutes ticked by and the John Collins were sunk. I was beginning to see things in a much rosier light.

'Christ!' I said. 'Even the first pair would seem beautiful to me now!'

The manager came running in. 'Me got girls! Me got girls! You like these – very much.'

We did, too. They looked like film starlets, the one on the left endowed like Jane Russell.

'Now that's really something,' enthused Kiwi, to the manager's delight. 'These have got tits!'

To prove it, he walked over to the two smiling, contoured girls and ran his hands over their taut breasts like a farmer running his hands over a cow at market. The girls did not bat an Oriental eyelid.

'What you think, Kingy?' he asked me, over his shoulder.

'Oh, yes,' I replied. 'I'll have her on the right!'

The black, smiling eyes in the impeccably made-up face of the girl I had selected flashed me a look of thank you and promise.

'That suits me fine,' said Kiwi, putting his arm round the trim waist of the bigger-titted girl. He led her over to the bar and the other girl came over and stood by me.

'These girls,' said the beaming manager, 'will be four thousand yen, please. Each. You have them three days they cost three thousand yen, each.'

'We'll pay one day for now and see how we go,' said Kiwi, and we gave the bowing manager the money.

In very good English my girl introduced herself as Suki and said that her friend's name was Inako.

'Could I have a John Collins?' she asked politely.

'Of course you can,' I said.

After taking a sip, leaving lipstick on the rim, she told me, seductively: 'I have had the operation on my eyes to make me look like a Western woman. Do you like my eyes?'

'Very much,' I said. 'You look like Hedy Lamarr, the film star.' And she laughed delightfully.

Moving closer to me, so that her warmth and perfume made me feel giddy, she said: 'I always dress Western world fashion. The Western world is very important to us. Do you like my dress?'

It was black and silky with a wide, black patent leather belt emphasising her tiny waist. The hem just brushed her knees. Her legs were long and slender.

'Very nice,' I said, hoarsely.

'Feel it,' she invited, lifting the hem.

I rubbed the material between thumb and forefinger.

Huskily, she went on: 'I love the feel of silk – my stockings – and, look . . .' she ran her cupped hand caressingly up her leg, the liquid movement taking the skirt and silk petticoat with it '. . . what do you think of these?'

My eyes had followed her hand up past her golden thighs, swelling above the convex of her stocking-tops, and came to rest on the edge of the sexiest black-lace knickers I had ever seen.

'Beautiful,' I breathed, reaching out a hand to touch them. She stood still for a moment while I touched her, looking at me tantalisingly, a glass in one hand and holding up her dress with the other.

'Let's go to bed,' I growled, impatiently.

She dropped the hem of her skirt, arching herself away from my hand, then came in close to me so that our bodies were touching.

'Later,' she whispered in my ear. 'There is plenty of time. I am your wife for twenty-four hours.'

She pressed herself even harder against me. 'I wish I could be your wife for longer,' she mewed.

'We'll see,' I promised her.

We saw that Kiwi and Inako were dancing to the soft music coming from the hidden speakers. Still holding her glass, Suki put her arms around my neck and swung her hips, sensuously.

'Dance?' she asked.

She was lithe like a cat and squirmed her body against me from her breasts to her knees. She nibbled the lobe of my ear. I dropped both hands and dug my fingers into the soft cheeks of her gyrating bottom, loving the feel of the silks rubbing against each other.

Then she looked steadily into my eyes. 'I think we *will* do as you suggested and go to bed now,' she said, eagerly. 'But first, I bath you.'

Excitedly, I called to Kiwi that we were going to the bath.

'We'll join you,' he said.

'Do we want drinks in our rooms?' asked Suki.

Kiwi and I looked at each other and nodded. Suki spoke to the barman in Japanese, then linked her arm through mine.

'OK,' she said. 'To the bath!'

The bathroom was all yellow-tiled with two sunken baths, already filled with steaming water, in the middle of the floor. Four large, white, fluffy towels lay folded on four chrome chairs and coat hangers hung from pegs on the wall.

Kiwi and I let the girls undress first, drooling over the double striptease. Naked, they walked down the sunken steps, Suki in one bath and Inako in the other.

Kiwi had all his clothes off in a trice and was in the water, hugging Inako by the time I'd got my boots off. Suki stood watching me undress, her head on one side.

'You have a very nice body,' she said, approvingly, as I put one big toe into the water. I drew my foot back quickly. The water was almost too hot to bear.

'Christ,' I said. 'I'm not getting into that!'

Suki laughed. 'Come on,' she said, softly. 'It's not that hot. Look.' She lowered herself down until her breasts were beneath the water and she was sitting on the bottom. I sat down on the tiled floor and gradually slid my feet into the water.

'Don't you find it too hot?' I asked Kiwi who was splashing merrily in the next bath.

'It's enough to sizzle your balls off. But who cares? Get in, you coward!'

Kiwi laughed. 'Do you know why they make us take hot baths, Kingy? Not to make us clean. Oh, no. It's to make us infertile. When the hot water touches your balls, the sperms just curl up and die. That's why you don't have to wear a French Letter. Bare-back all the way. Ain't that a fact, Inako?'

Giggling, she pushed him down under the water.

My face took on a look of anticipated agony and I lowered myself into the bath. After a while I found it wasn't too bad at all.

'Suki,' I ventured, 'is it true what Kiwi said about the hot water and not having to take precautions?'

She smiled at me with deep affection. 'Yes,' she replied, 'we will be like man and wife in the bed.'

Knowing what her words signified and seeing her clean-cut limbs and body I cupped her pear-shaped breasts then let my hands slide down to her waist and out round the curve of her hips. As I brought my hands forward to the middle, she slapped them away.

'No!' she said. 'In the bath, we bath.' Then she smiled. 'The bed is for that,' she added, softly. 'You be a good boy.'

She picked up the soap and lathered me all over thoroughly.

'Now, you wash me,' she said, handing me the soap. 'And that is all.'

101

The girls got out first, leaving us to soak while they dried themselves. Then they spread their towels for us to step on to and wrapped fresh ones round our bodies.

'Oh, boy,' groaned Kiwi. 'I do feel sick. Here's me with a gorgeous girl and all I can think about and taste is fish eyeballs!'

'You'll be all right when you get another drink down you,' I tried to pacify him.

In our bedroom, Suki asked me: 'Would you like some pyjamas? I have some silk ones in my case.' She giggled. 'They are bright yellow, but I like a man in pyjamas.'

'If that's how you like your men, OK.'

She handed me the pyjamas, then let her bath towel slip to the floor. She put on a black silk nightie. I whistled as she stepped in front of the beside light which made the silk transparent. The nightie was deep-cut to her waist, each side of it cupping a breast.

We got into bed and sat, sipping our drinks and intertwining our toes.

'Are you really a princess?' I asked, in all innocence. 'The manager said you were.'

This amused her very much. 'I am a shorthand typist,' she said. 'A secretary.'

'Then what on earth are you doing here?'

'I am on holiday. Most girls who work in Tokyo do this sort of thing during vacations. It gives us extra money.'

'Christ, I can't imagine English secretaries doing it.'

'That is because it is not recognised in your country.'

'Do you enjoy it?'

'Sometimes – I shall with you.'

'Does your boss know what you're doing?'

'Oh, yes. Every girl in our office does it. Inako works with me.'

I shook my head. 'I just can't get over it.'

'It is only in Tokyo and the big towns that there is money. In the country the people are very poor. Peasants, you call them. My family is very poor. I have nine brothers and sisters, and I send money home to them. I am the eldest. I am not a prostitute. I enjoy pleasing men, and I enjoy love-making. When my holiday is over in a week's time I shall go back to work.'

'What were you doing at eleven-thirty last night?'

'Sipping tea and wondering if I would get a phone call. Why?'

I told her about my thoughts in the plane. She was delighted.

'And what do you think about the girl you had never met before and now you are in bed with?'

'Terrific!' I replied, in all honesty.

She took my empty glass and put it with her own on the floor. Then she pulled the top of her nightdress wider apart so that her breasts slipped out, and pushed a nipple between my lips.

'And now I shall truly be a wife to you,' she said.

I awoke at dawn to find there were two more hands in the bed, caressing me from behind. I turned over, out of the arms of the sleeping Suki and into the arms of a wide-awake Inako!

'Your friend is ill,' she whispered. 'He sick all over me. So I bathe again and come to your bed. He sleeping now.'

She tugged my shoulder. 'It's all right. Suki won't mind.'

She didn't either. In fact she joined in the action!

The sun was streaming through the window when I awoke again at ten thirty. I had a slight hangover and I felt sick at the sight of Japanese women. The air reeked of staleness, garlic and hair lacquer. I crawled from the bed, draped a towel round me, grabbed my clothes and went next door to see Kiwi. The stench of vomit in his room was worse.

'Boy!' he mumbled, when he finally came round. 'Do I feel terrible? Terrible! Just terrible!'

'How about some nice fish eyeballs and rice?' I asked him.

He, too, had had enough of Japanese women and we decided to ditch the girls and sneak out without waking them. We went to the bathroom, washed and dressed hurriedly and left the hotel. We found a café and had breakfast. At least, I did. Kiwi just had coffee – black. Afterwards, we strolled along in the sunshine and began to feel drowsy.

103

'Let's find a park and have a sleep,' suggested Kiwi. 'It's too early for drinking.'

We arrived at a huge, immaculately kept park with a moat-like stream and living miniatures of trees from almost every temperate clime. In particular I liked the oaks and elms. High, spiked railings enclosed the park but we discovered a small gate that was unlocked, and went inside.

There were real-size trees as well and we sat down in the shade of a conifer. I took out my pay-book, counted 4,000 yen and handed them to Kiwi.

'What's that for?' he asked.

I told him about Inako. He burst out laughing. 'Hell! I don't want that!' he said, thrusting the money back. 'Have that one on me.' He shook his head, still chuckling. 'Well, whadyer know about that.'

'You'll have to make up for it tonight,' I said with a grin.

We closed our eyes. It was peaceful and quiet save for the distant rumble of traffic which helped to lull us into a very deep sleep.

We were awakened by an urgent Japanese voice, speaking English. 'Get up! Get up! Get out of here at once!'

Two Japanese men were bending over us. One wore the clothes of a gardener, the other the street clothes of a London barrister. Gardener clutched a garden rake, barrister was the spokesman.

'Why? What's the matter?' I asked, sitting up.

'Is there a fire, or something?' Kiwi joined in.

Barrister's voice was hissing reverence: 'Don't you realise where you are? You are in the Emperor's palace grounds. Leave at once or I will have you arrested!'

'All right, all right,' I growled as Kiwi and I got to our feet. 'Keep your hair on.' Then Kiwi and I both laughed when we noticed that he looked like Yul Brynner! Gardener and barrister stepped back a couple of paces.

'Leave at once! Leave at once!' The voice was near to hysteria.

'OK. We're going,' I said. 'But remember, you bastards killed and tortured lots of Englishmen in the last war, so don't make me lose my temper.'

Kiwi and I walked to the gate and they followed at a discreet distance. As the gate was locked behind us, Kiwi and I told them in no uncertain terms what we thought of Hirohito.

We spent the rest of the day sight-seeing and drinking. Then I saw that Kay Starr was on at the Tokyo Casino.

'Now that's a girl I could really go to bed with,' I said. 'That song of hers, "Till I Meet You Once Again", really gets me going.'

'Let's go, then,' said Kiwi.

We managed to book two seats in the second row for the second house that night. Then we did some serious drinking until the performance started. We also spent the entire interval in the theatre bar, and returned to our seats ready for anything.

Up went the curtain and on to the stage came real French-style can-can girls, their white, flared-legged knickers leaving little to the imagination during the high kicks.

'Yippee!' we yelled along with scores of other soldiers.

At the end of the dance, the compère asked if there were any soldiers from Korea who would like to can-can with the girls. Kiwi and I, needing no second invite, ran up the steps on to the stage and we each grabbed a girl by the waist.

The compère waggled a finger at us. 'Naughty, naughty,' he admonished us. He turned back to the microphone: 'Come on, there must be more of you out there!' He looked behind and saw that Kiwi and I were twanging the girls' long, black suspenders. 'Look how they're enjoying themselves!'

After persuasion, he managed to get eight more soldiers up on to the stage – one for each girl.

'Right,' he said, 'take your cue from your two friends and hold your girl round the waist. OK? A few practice steps first.'

The music started up and, to us – and the audience – it was the best part of the show so far. Army boots were never meant to dance in. The lively can-can music was punctuated by the drum-beat thuds of boots on boards. Now and then a higher note in the can-can girls' screams could be heard as a thick sole landed on a vulnerable high-heeled shoe.

The dance was one of my most memorable and happy

moments. I didn't know which pair of shapely, dancing thighs to look at – those on my right or those on my left.

'Christ, I'm sweating!' I yelled to Kiwi. 'And just look at this bitch go!'

My girl had turned slightly sideways towards me and was high-kicking so that her ankle brushed my nose.

'Time we got a souvenir!' Kiwi yelled back at me. 'Grab her knickers!'

I caught the girl's ankle as it came level with my eyes and clutched her knickers with my other hand. The girl yelped as she lost her balance and fell backwards, leaving her ripped undergarment in my hand.

'Yippee!' I cried, waving them aloft.

As the girl fell, she knocked over Kiwi and his girl. He promptly started to rip his partner's knickers off as well. The other soldiers were quick to catch on. Screaming and pandemonium broke out and, to the accompaniment of delighted hoots and whistles from the audience, eight more girls were de-knickered, and the curtain was brought down.

The girls and management took it all with forced pleasantness. They also took back all the knickers. We went back to our seats to enjoy the rest of the show and the singing of beautiful Kay Starr. To my delight, her finale was 'Till I Meet You Once Again'.

It was two nights and four girls later that Kiwi and I met the Australian in a bar. He was unshaven, inebriated and his bootlaces were undone.

'Hey, Aussie,' Kiwi called to him. 'You'll break your neck if you don't do up your boots.'

He came stomping over to us. 'I don't want to die with my boots on,' he slurred, near to tears. 'That's why I never do them up. Then I can get them off quick. I don't want to die with them on.'

It seemed to me that many Australian soldiers shared a complex about dying with their boots on.

Aussie sat down on a chair next to us, lifted up his foot and slipped his boot off.

'There,' he said, seriously. 'See how easily they come off?'

I ignored the slightly radiating sock and asked: 'On your own?'

He peered all round the bar. 'Yep,' he said, finally, 'the bastards seem to have left me. What say I join you?'

'Suits us,' said Kiwi.

Aussie lurched off to the bar and came back with three beers. We began swapping yarns about Korea and soon Kiwi and I were feeling nice and merry. But no matter how much beer Aussie put away, he didn't get any drunker.

The door opened and his lost mates came in – two Australians and two chunky Maoris.

'Come on, mate,' said one of the Australians, dropping a hand on Aussie's shoulder, 'we're going to get Maori, here, a doll off a Christmas tree.'

'What are you talking about?' blurted Aussie. 'It's nowhere near Christmas.'

'It's less than two months away,' replied the Australian. 'Lissen, there's this restaurant down the road that's got a big, big tree in one corner, and Maori wants the doll off the top of it.'

'Tell Maori to buy it. Go on, Maori, you buy it. Here — ' Aussie put his hand in his pocket for some money.

'He can't,' cut in the Australian, 'the fucking bastard of a restaurant owner won't let him have it – so we're going to take it.'

'Why didn't you say so in the first place?' said Aussie. 'My two friends here will help.'

'Sure we will,' I said.

The three of us drained our glasses then we all trooped down the road to the restaurant. Music was coming from a jukebox and Japanese couples were dancing. As we burst in, the dancing stopped. Grim-faced waiters formed behind the manager who came hurrying over to us.

'You no come looking for trouble here,' he said. 'We no like soldiers. You go or me call MPs.'

'Pleasant, ain't he?' said one of the Australians.

The other stepped close up to the manager. 'All we want is the doll off the Christmas tree. Maori, here, wants it for

107

his little girl back home. Now come on, be reasonable, how much do you want for it?'

'You go, please,' demanded the manager.

'Why, you mangy little — ' The Australian didn't wait to complete the description. He hit the manager in the side of the neck with his fist. The manager went down, gurgling.

The waiters instantly shouted and jumped on us. The diners rushed from their tables and stood as far away as possible, together with the couples who had been dancing.

The two Maoris threw the waiters off like water from a duck's back and formed a spearhead to rush for the tree. A waiter was trying to twist Kiwi's arm completely off when I sunk my boot into his backside. The waiter turned, in pain, and received my elbow between his eyes. He went down without a murmur.

As the Maoris forged ahead to the tree, one Australian went down under three waiters. I clasped my hands and brought them down on the back of the neck of one of them. Aussie leapt into the air, leaving one unlaced boot behind, and landed on the back of a second. The third twisted and crouched, judo-fashion.

'Ho, ho, what have we here?' I asked.

The waiter began dancing from one foot to the other, eyeing both Kiwi and me in turn.

'Stand still, you bastard,' I said, 'and let me hit you.'

The waiter had forgotten about the Australian, who had rolled away and picked up a chair. Everything suddenly went black for the waiter as one leg of the chair caught him across his right ear.

Kiwi dashed to the second waiter who had somehow got on top of Aussie, yanked his head back by the hair and knocked him flat with a wide swing to the side of the jaw. Aussie thanked Kiwi, found his boot and put it on.

By now the others were at the tree. Kiwi and I ran to them.

'Pull the tree over,' cried a Maori. Kiwi and I grabbed a lower branch and wrenched. The tree crashed down to land on the jukebox, ending the record with a long, dying squeal.

The Maori who wanted the doll plucked it off the top of

the tree, gave an ear-splitting war whoop and headed for the door, the remaining waiters falling back, resignedly, to allow us to follow.

Outside, we ran for all we were worth and cut up a side street. We stopped, puffing and laughing victoriously.

'I think we should split up, just in case the MPs come snooping,' said one Australian. We all agreed.

'Thanks for your help, mates,' the Australian added, and Kiwi and I were on our own again.

We kept walking along the side street. Several children came up to us. 'You want bang-cracker?' they chorused, showing us a bag of small, silver-paper balls.

'What the devil have you got there?' Kiwi asked them.

One of the boys placed a silver ball on the pavement and stamped on it. It went off with quite a loud crack.

'You make plenty bang,' he said. 'Put on table, hit with hand. Frighten people in restaurant.'

'Hey, that's not a bad idea,' I said. 'What are they made of?'

The boy handed me one. I found it was hollow and contained two pieces of grit and two caps.

'Pretty good,' said Kiwi. 'How much?'

The boy held up the bag. 'Hundred and fifty yen.'

Kiwi gave him the money and took the bag. 'Now we'll have some fun,' he said, chortling.

We experimented with the balls and found that the sides of our fists were painless detonators. We headed down to the main road and went into a dimly lit bar on the corner.

Inside were several Australians, sitting round a table, drinking and talking to four Japanese girls. The smiling barmaids were leaning over the bar-top.

The Australians paid little attention to us as we walked in and ordered two beers. We each placed about six silver balls on the counter and banged them off in quick succession.

One of the Australians shrieked and dived under the table; the girls screamed and the other Australians instinctively ducked. Our laughter was short-lived.

'You pommy bastards!' one Australian roared, ignoring the fact that Kiwi was a New Zealander. 'We've got a cobber here who's just getting over shell-shock. Get out, you pommy bastards!'

The Australians converged on us. We tried to put up a reluctant fight but there were too many of them. We found ourselves thrown bodily outside and into the gutter.

'And if you want to come back with some of your pommy bastard friends,' shouted an Australian, 'we'll be waiting for you.'

We sat in the gutter, looking at ourselves after the Australians had gone back into the bar.

'Well,' I said, getting to my feet, 'that wasn't exactly what I'd call a success.'

'I've a good mind to go back in there and let some more off,' declared Kiwi, belligerently.

I shook my head. 'They might not be so nice to us next time. Besides, I feel pretty awful about that bloke with shell-shock. It's a terrible thing.'

So, with the silver ball bangers in our pockets, we set off to find more complacent victims.

We banged the silver balls on the pavements, bringing jumps – with smiles or snarls – from different people; we caused havoc in a select Japanese bar, and we frightened passengers out of their wits on Tokyo's Underground. It was absolute bliss, making bangs without the fear of being shot back at.

About midnight, when we were standing on the pavement, wondering what to do now that the silver balls had all gone, a pimp taxi-driver drew up.

'You want girls? Me take you very nice place.'

We instantly piled into the back.

'Drive on, McDuff,' I told him, 'and no more than ninety up the High Street!'

'Where the bloody hell's he taking us?' asked Kiwi as the street lights became fewer.

'Probably to have our throats cut,' I said with a grin.

The taxi swung round the side of a park, turned left and stopped outside a large, four-storey house standing in its own grounds with tall trees all round it. There were no lights.

'Christ, what is this?' I asked. 'The morgue?'

110

The taxi-driver smiled. 'You get lovely girls here. I show.'

He opened a wrought-iron gate and we followed him up the paved garden path. He knocked on the heavy door. We heard the movement of a window above and stepped back to look up. A beautiful Eurasian woman was looking down from a now open and lighted window. A string of foreign words flowed between her and the taxi-driver. Then she disappeared. A minute later, the door opened and we were ushered inside.

The woman shut the door and switched on a light.

'We're in a fucking brothel!' Kiwi whispered to me, needlessly.

The large hall we were in left no doubt about that. The walls were adorned with paintings and statuettes of Japanese couples in different positions of copulation.

The woman said something else to the taxi-driver, then spoke to us in English: 'I have only two girls left tonight. You wish to see?'

We nodded. She led us up the winding staircase, opened up a small bar – the décor of which continued the theme in the hall – and left us with drinks. I asked the taxi-driver to wait.

The passing of minutes went almost unnoticed as we studied the works of erotic art. The woman returned with two sleepy-looking Japanese girls. One was slim and very attractive. The other resembled a mountain of lard.

'You can have the slim one,' I said to Kiwi.

He looked at the fat one and winced. 'Hell! You're not going to bed with that?'

'Of course not!'

'Well, what are you going to do?'

'You never mind about me. I know what I'm doing. You just pay for your one and take her away.'

'Yes, but . . .' He caught my wink and shrugged.

'OK,' he said, and turned to the Eurasian. 'How much for her?'

'Three thousand yen.'

Kiwi counted out the money. 'Come on, honey,' he told the girl. 'I'm mighty tired.'

'You want this girl?' asked the Eurasian when Kiwi and the slim one had gone.

'No,' I replied. 'I want you.'

I had been studying the Eurasian from the moment I first saw her. She was about thirty to thirty-five, I guessed, and very beautiful indeed. She looked completely boneless, and she put curves into her straight-cut silk kimono. Her eyes were wide-set and like black almonds. Her hair, the same colour, was drawn back into a sleek chignon.

'Impossible!' she cried. 'I am not for sale. This is my house!'

'Well, I certainly don't want that,' I said, nodding towards the fat girl. 'And if I can't have you, I'll go.'

'I am sorry,' was all she said, dismissively.

I turned to the taxi-driver. 'Take me back to town.'

I was just getting into the taxi when the upstairs window went up.

'Soldier!' she called. 'Will you come back, please?'

Grinning broadly, I paid off the taxi-driver. 'You were right about getting a lovely girl,' I said.

She was waiting for me at the door and I followed her up the stairs and into the bar. She looked at me steadily and without warmth.

'All right,' she said, flatly, and left the room. She returned carrying a silk dressing gown.

'Here,' she said, handing it to me. 'Come along.'

I followed her along a corridor, doubly excited at not knowing quite what was in store.

'Bathroom,' she said, opening a door. 'You come across to this room afterwards.' She pointed to another door.

'Aren't you going to bath me?' I asked.

Her eyes almost smiled. 'No. I bath alone.'

'Ah, well,' I thought, when I was in the bath, 'at least I can have the bloody water at the temperature I want!'

I wallowed and felt good. After drying myself quickly I put on the dressing gown. Folding my clothes neatly in a pile, I carried them across to the other room and knocked lightly on the door.

'It's not locked,' she called.

As I walked in she rose from the bed where she had been sitting. Her perfume wafted to me like honeysuckle. She indicated that I put my clothes on to a chair. I did so and turned to face her.

The almond-shaped eyes were black, deep and smiling. Her lips were suggestively parted. She had undone the chignon. The hard-brushed tresses hung to below her shoulders. She was wearing a dressing gown similar to mine but with frills.

Slowly and deliberately she opened it wide. I drew in my breath sharply. She was naked except for long, black nylon stockings held up by frilly red garters. Her feet were displayed in gold-coloured, heeled sandals, the red varnish on her toenails showing through the sheer nylon. Her body was golden brown and smooth.

I had never seen breasts so large and pointed. They stood erect with their fullness. I liked the way her tummy tucked itself in at the navel then rounded out slightly to dip again. I liked everything. She was magnificent.

I went to her and crushed her down on to the bed. She was like warm, vibrant foam rubber.

'No,' she said, pushing me over on to my back. 'Not yet. I like to enjoy the pleasure, too. I will teach you how a man should really make love to a woman.'

She turned herself so that her nyloned thighs were lying close to my head, and then her lips were tickling their way down my belly.

I jumped as a thrill shot through my body. How much more intimate than the Kowloon café experience! The sensation was excruciatingly delicious. I looked at the gartered thighs so close to my head and the black hair above them. Tentatively I put my nose to the hair. It was soft and smelled of perfume. I heard her groan and she parted her thighs. The desire coursing through me dispensed with inhibitions. I put my mouth to her. It was the first time I had ever done such a thing. Surprisingly, there was no taste. It was just like kissing a woman on the mouth but, oh, so much, much more intimate.

Her mouth worked faster. It was a warm, encompassing

113

tunnel of comfort and safety and my whole being felt as though it were inside it. My desire became almost unbearable. Her hips were heaving, and I began thrusting my own hips and tongue in unison.

Suddenly her legs stiffened and crossed themselves at the ankles, causing her thighs to press themselves against my ears. At the same time she pressed herself hard against my mouth. She gripped my hair and caressed my head with frenzied hands and screamed something in her own language. She began to gasp. The gasps changed into a long, kittenish wail. Then she was still and silent.

I lay for a while, stroking her thighs. Then she sat up. Her eyes were blacker, and sleepy with almost a drugged look.

'That was nice, eh?' she asked.

'Mmm!' I murmured.

She got off the bed and meticulously pulled her stockings taut and adjusted the red garters. She fetched two cigarettes, lit them both with an ornately carved table lighter and placed one between my lips.

'Thank you,' I said, taking a long drag. 'If it's not asking too much,' I ventured, 'could I possibly have a drink?'

She nodded. 'What would you like?'

'John Collins, please.'

She bent and kissed me full on the lips, then turned from the bed and buttoned her dressing gown. When she had gone, I could still see her beautiful body in my mind.

She returned with two drinks. Taking off her dressing gown, she sat down on the bed next to me, her shoulders and thighs touching mine.

'Cheers!' she said, lifting her glass.

Her eyes had lost their drugged look. They sparkled and were full of merriment. There was something else in them, too. The look of a very successful, masterful teacher – a teacher sure of her pupil.

'Cheers!' I replied.

We sipped our drinks quietly. Almost imperceptibly at first, she began rubbing her thigh against mine. Then she lifted her leg, sensuously, and laid it over mine, rubbing her nyloned calf up and down the inside of my leg.

114

Her eyes were laughing now, and full of mischief. She can do as she likes with me, I thought, and she knows it.

She looked down at me with a mocking message that she would have to do something by way of resuscitation.

As her head moved slowly towards mine, slowly, her mouth began opening. Her tongue was flicking through as her lips touched mine.

'There!' she breathed into my mouth. Our empty glasses fell with a muffled clunk on to the carpet. She fell back, pulling me with her and on top of her, and once more I entered a tunnel of heavenly deliciousness, and her arms and legs crossed themselves above me.

'Well,' I said to Kiwi, as we were riding back to town in a taxi the following mid-morning, 'I have read a lot about that sort of thing in books – you know, some of these authors euphemise orgasm as the earth, moon and stars fusing together, or waves crashing on to the shore and rocks with crescendo, with a bit of thunder and lightning thrown in for good measure – but do you know how I'd describe last night?'

He shook his head. 'Tell me.'

'I'd say it felt as if all my fucking guts were coming out!'

Kiwi guffawed. 'The trouble with you, Kingy, is that you've got no soul – no poetry. You're just a Philistine. Still, I'll say this much for you – you did get to shack up with the most beautiful momma of the house – and for free, at that. I've never heard of that happening before. How did you do it?'

'I didn't do anything,' I said, modestly. 'She told me she'd never made love to a red-haired man before and she wanted the experience. And you should have seen the huge breakfast she gave me.'

'Don't talk about food – I'm starving!'

To take his mind off his empty stomach, we laughed and talked some more about the way authors hid behind a bushel when describing the sex act, and we made a few suggestions of our own.

'How about: "He roared up her like an express train and fired both balls at once",' I said.

'Yeah, or: "He was lucky he was anchored by his big Army boots"!'

'One of the best ways I've heard it described is in "Eskimo Nell",' I told him.

'What's that? A book?'

'No, it's a poem. You've never heard it? When Dead-Eyed Dick and Mexican Pete, Go out in search of fun, It's Dead-Eyed Dick who swings the prick, And Mexican Pete the gun.'

'Do you know any more?'

I recited as much as I knew. 'That's great,' he said. 'I'll have to write down the words. The boys will be tickled pink.'

On the night before we were due to fly back to Korea, Kiwi became edgy and decided to return to Camp Ebisu. I didn't bother to argue with him.

'OK, if that's what you want. I'll see you back at Seoul about tea-time tomorrow. I shan't go back to camp until my leave's up at ten o'clock tomorrow morning.'

I joined up with some English soldiers for a long drinking bout. Just after two o'clock in the morning I found I had close on seven thousand yen left and decided to find myself a girl. I thought about going to see the Eurasian, but I hadn't a clue where she lived or where we had been when the pimp taxi-driver had found us.

I left the group and lurched rather hazily along the pavement. Later, I remembered being stopped by a rather trim green coat and six-inch high heels and going off to a hotel room. I vaguely remember the girl's efforts to get me to make love to her, and that was all.

I awoke at first light to find myself alone in a crumpled bed. My first thoughts were for my money. I took my pay book from my tunic pocket and found that only two thousand, five hundred yen had been taken. In their place was a piece of paper with the words 'Thank you' written in pencil.

A warm feeling towards human nature swept over me. I wanted to find the girl and give her all my money for her honesty. It was something I knew from bitter experience that no London prostitute would have done. Not only would she have taken all my money but she'd have had her pimp throw me out into the gutter as well.

Then the sad, deflating thought hit me that the short, whirlwind leave of fornication, drinking and merriment was over. Back to the jaws of death. Still, I hadn't done too badly. I'd had four women that I could remember in four days, and one that I couldn't picture at all.

But I hadn't sent Sylvia or Mum a souvenir, and I decided to say nothing about Tokyo to them. Guilt descended on me.

When I boarded the Globemaster I felt as sick, miserable and desperately resigned to death as I had done when I'd watched England slip away out of sight. What price glory now, I asked myself. I must have been nuts to have wanted it in the first place. Why the devil hadn't I stayed on the farm? After all, horses' backsides weren't such a terrible sight.

I sat in the plane, not bothering to join in any conversation. I felt alone and terribly homesick. I yearned to be going to England and to find my old job on the farm waiting for me.

After two hours of flight, I drifted into sleep and dreamt I was on the same plane.

One after the other, its four engines coughed and stopped. The nose of the plane dipped sharply and the mountains of Korea came hurtling up to us.

There was no escape. This was it, this time. I set my heels against the base of the seat in front and clasped my hands behind my neck as I had been taught.

I jerked awake and my panic eased for a split second with relief that I had been only dreaming.

Then reality crashed in! I was still on the bloody plane!

The remaining two and a half hours of flight time were equally nightmarish. I rode them out, neurotically tuned for the slightest splutter or note-change from an engine.

Not even in Korea had I felt so depressed and frightened.

11

That the North Koreans were determined not to give anyone any rest for reclaiming The Hook was evident by the welcome I received on rejoining the troop. Shells were continually coming in, many of them skimming the top of the hill and landing among the mortars tucked in behind.

I thought how Alabama had been right about the worst part of R-and-R being the return to the front line. I felt like a new boy all over again and found myself ducking needlessly. For the first two days I had the jitters. Adding to my maladjustment was the fact that there were no letters from Sylvia or Mum.

It was strange, too, being without Stan and Leggy. They had departed for Tokyo on the day I left the lustful capital. The whole troop looked battle-weary and no one was very interested in hearing of my exploits, still very fresh in my mind. If there is an expression meaning culture shock in reverse, I had it!

I mooched about and was more than eager to help out in the command post. When I wasn't on duty I slept most of the time and, thankfully, Sergeant-Major Winscombe let me be. On my third night back from Tokyo something happened which restored my self-confidence and the 'up-and-at-'em' spirit.

There was a heavy black layer of cloud over the area, completely blocking out the stars and moon, though the latter was trying to penetrate the weaker places. Because of atmospherics on the radio it was impossible to contact the Turkish unit a few miles away.

Lieutenant Robb, who looked like a dapper Frenchman with his trim hair-line moustache and Roman nose, came to my dug-out.

'I know it's pretty dark, Gerald,' he said, 'but would you take an important message to the Turks? Charles can go with you.'

Charles was the command post's TARA. His father was a colonel and he had 'let down the family tradition' by failing WOSB – the War Office Selection Board for officers. He had a thick black moustache and a wide gap between his two upper front teeth, and looked not unlike Terry-Thomas. He even had the voice and mannerisms of the comedian.

But if Charles didn't have what it takes to be an officer, he certainly wasn't lacking in bravery. One night, when the enemy had got too close to the mortars for comfort, he came down from the ridge, his rifle piping hot, and exclaimed to me: 'My deah chap, one could positively – but *positively* – get killed up there! Those nasty little bullets are like hornets!'

Like me, he loved words. He also liked to invent the most subtle of jokes and he had a keen wit.

We climbed into the F-O-P jeep and I drove off – without lights and with the windscreen down, into the black night.

'Deah chap,' he said, 'you'll do your best to keep on the road, won't you?'

'Don't worry,' I told him. 'The road is always just a shade lighter than the sides.'

'I would have used the word "nuance" for the difference, but I don't think this particular road appreciates what you said.'

'What did you say your guide dog's name was?' I retorted.

We crossed a plain that we knew was in full view of the enemy and reached the Turks without mishap – only to be almost shot.

I stopped the jeep in the road and Charles, clutching the buff-coloured envelope, started walking up the short hill towards the dark figures of two sentries, who instantly raised their rifles and let forth a stream of Turkish.

'What *are* the idiots blathering about?' demanded Charles, and continued walking.

'The password, Charles!' I yelled. 'Give them the second part of the password!'

119

'What is it?' he asked, blandly, as the sentries, still bellowing Turkish, took aim.

'Christ!' I exclaimed, then yelled: 'Horse!' This complemented the word 'Trojan'. The sentries lowered their rifles.

Waving the envelope as he walked by the two sentries, Charles told them: 'You really *must* learn to speak English.'

Message delivered, we started back. Whatever misty rays the moon had been able to send through the cloud suddenly stopped when we reached the plain, and it was blacker than ever.

'I will sit on the bonnet,' said Charles, with initiative, 'and direct you by calling out "left" or "right". Deah chap, you do know which is your left and your right?'

'You, Charles, are the ciliated epithelium of a woman's oviduct.'

'Don't be indelicate,' he replied. 'Besides, *that* is useful. Which is more than you are!'

But Charles couldn't see any better than I could. After a few yards of 'Left! No! Right!' the nearside wheels dropped into a fairly deep ditch. Charles hit the ground with a yelp and a thud, and the engine cut out. And it refused to start again.

'What have you done?' he accused. 'Apart from almost breaking my neck. Why won't it start?'

'Because,' I informed him, patiently, 'the carburettor is at too much of an angle to function.'

'Then what are you going to do? I don't fancy walking. And what are you doing now?'

'Taking my boot off.'

'Taking your boot . . . ?' Words failed him. 'All I really needed, just to make my life that little bit more complete, was to be stranded, close to the enemy in the black of night, with a lunatic who wants to cavort, bare-footed, through the toadstools!'

'Just shut up a minute.'

I removed my long, woollen Army sock, took off the petrol cap and dipped my sock down the tube.

'We have to put petrol into the carburettor,' I explained. 'Lift the bonnet and take the air filter pipe off.'

'Are you sure that a volatile liquid, mixed with a sweaty sock that is probably capable of walking on its own, is fully recommended by the manufacturer?'

It was then that Sod's Law took a hand. The black layer of cloud suddenly broke and we were flooded by moonlight.

'I think we are what is called spotlighted,' said Charles.

'I think we are in the shit,' I responded.

'I think you are probably right. Let's be rather quick, eh?'

I was squeezing the petrol from my sock into the carburettor when bullets ricocheted, screaming, from the road close by us, making us both jump.

'I say!' declared Charles. 'That's not at all sporting, shooting at us with rifles when we are handicapped like this.'

As though the North Koreans had heard his words, the bullets stopped – and two mortars burst on the road about fifty yards ahead of us.

'Drop fifty – and we've had it,' said Charles, quietly.

I pulled the starter. The engine tried to fire but there wasn't enough petrol. As I dipped my sock a second time, with trembling fingers, two mortars burst behind us.

'They are not very good, are they?' commented Charles. 'I estimate that with corrections and time of flight, we have a maximum of thirty seconds in which to get the hell out of here, with or without the jeep!'

'You squeeze in the petrol while I pull the starter!' I told him.

This time, the engine started and, hoping that Charles would get out of the way, I tore out of the ditch before the supplementary petrol burned up or evaporated. I braked and the bonnet slammed down; Charles leapt in and we were away!

As I was swerving to avoid the first volley's craters, a third pair of mortars flashed and cracked just about where the jeep had been.

'That was exceeding close,' observed Charles, letting out his breath.

When we were out of the danger zone I slowed and said to Charles: 'It was really good having you by my side. You

121

really are a great guy. I couldn't think of a nicer person to die with.'

'Thank you – and, ditto.'

'Do you know, Charles, I made a big resolution back there.'

'And what "big" – terrible word usage – resolution did the excuses for cerebral cells in the head of the mighty Hiawatha manage to manufacture, pray tell me?'

'That if I get out of Korea alive, I will never again complain, no matter what predicament I find myself in: such as changing a flat tyre in freezing rain, running out of petrol in the middle of nowhere, getting stranded on a cheerless railway station in the dead of night with no more trains till morning, being broke, cold and hungry. I will always remember tonight and comfort myself by saying: "Well, at least you're not being shot at, so why worry?".'

'I think that's a very good resolution, but it might be difficult to keep. I agree, too, that it *was* rather nerve-racking, waiting for those mortars to land. If I had two pips instead of two stripes, Gerald, I would have no hesitation in recommending you for a medal for the way you got us out of there.'

(If you are reading this, Charles, I would like to say that I *have* kept that resolution and it has served me well many times.)

Three days later, Stan and Leggy returned, and that night Stan and I sat in our dug-out, drinking beer and swapping stories of Tokyo. I could tell, though, he was as jittery and disconsolate as I had been. And he didn't get the opportunity to acclimatise to battle at the mortar end, as I had done. Next day we set off for the F-O-P. With us was Scouse's replacement, a strongly-accented Glaswegian called Gunner Jock McEwell.

'The heathen savages are beginning to multiply,' commented Stan.

Dog Troop's F-O-P men had had a really tough time the night before. We found that dug-outs were caved in and the

122

F-O-P was a shambles. Throughout the first night, we dug and dug and dug. By morning we were better entrenched than ever before. The Marines just didn't believe in digging and kept their trenches shallow.

In the evening, Alabama joined me and I regaled him with my Tokyo adventures. He looked tired and drawn, unshaven and probably unwashed. His combat suit was crumpled and soiled. But he still managed a grin or two.

The North Koreans were still throwing the shells in. Hardly an hour went by without one or two falling.

'I still can't decide which is worse,' I said to Alabama, 'having been with the shelling all the time or coming back to it after leave.'

'Speaking for myself, I think it's worse having been here all the time. It's getting more than flesh and blood can stand, man. More than flesh and blood can stand. I'm pretty tired. We all are. At least you've had a rest, giving your nerves and body time to freshen up.'

But next morning I found that my body had also had time for something else! I awoke, bursting, and ran to the 'benghazi' – a pipe sunk into the ground – to empty my bladder. And out came the proverbial 'razor blades'!

At the same time, five planes came zooming in. I stood there with my aching sapling in my hand, watching them. I suddenly realised they were coming straight at me!

'Christ! They're MIGs!' I shouted.

Then I caught sight of the white stars on their underwings. They swooped on over me to a small hill several hundred yards behind which was occupied by a unit of Royal Engineers. And then the HEs were dropping. The Americans were bombing the wrong hill!

The hill blurred as the bombs crashed on to the Engineers, killing eight and injuring many more.

What a bloody way to go, I thought. There were excruciating stabbing pains in my sapling and I felt inclined to blame those on to the Americans as well.

The US Airforce went further down the scale in our estimation. But I had a much, much more personal problem. The sapling was stinging all day. I confided in Stan.

'You've got a dose, you dirty bastard!' he said, confirming my fears. 'Keep away from me!'

Word soon got round about my condition. I was met by good-humoured chants of 'Unclean! Unclean!' from the Marines. The two Jocks even went so far as to serenade me:

> Off to the doctor's I did go,
> Doodah, doodah!
> Pimpled balls I had to show,
> Doodah, doodah day!
> In came a nurse with a red-hot lance,
> Doodah, doodah!
> Now you bugger I'll make you dance,
> Doodah, doodah day!

That evening there was sufficient starlight for me to take the jeep to see the medical captain at Battery HQ.

'Drop your trousers and let's have a look at it,' he said, phlegmatically.

He wasn't going to touch it. He took his baton and lifted it up. Obligingly, a green exudation appeared.

The captain sighed. 'You've got gonorrhoea,' he said, rubbing his baton vigorously with spirits.

'Local?' he asked.

'Tokyo,' I replied, quietly, wondering which of the women had given it to me.

'Well, you boys must have your fun, I suppose. You no doubt earnt it.'

The captain filled a hypodermic. 'Just bend over, will you?' Conversationally, he went on: 'The Australians are the worst. They're real terrors. They treat it like a cold in the nose. Very fond of spreading it, too. Injection one day and out with Korean girls the next.'

I hardly felt the needle but the penicillin going in was agony.

'You can dress yourself now. Whereabouts are you?'

'The Hook,' I said.

'Ah, well, I needn't tell you to keep away from women for ten days. Ha, ha!'

A few days later the Marines were relieved by the Black Watch. It happened so suddenly that I didn't get the chance to say cheerio to Alabama.

'Now we're really outnumbered!' said Stan.

But when the two Jocks went to see their own kind, they came back very disgruntled. 'Black Watch, did you say? Huh! That's a laugh. They're nearly all English!'

The Black Watch started off very badly in the line. They lost quite a few men on patrols out through no-man's-land and beyond, and they became trigger happy.

The dreadful word went round that in anger they had shot and killed a North Korean priest and ambulance men who were collecting their dead.

'They are saying that the priest and ambulance men were a patrol in disguise,' said Jock McCleod. 'It's a favourite trick of Chinky.'

I didn't know who to believe. I didn't have much time for any infantry regiment from the British Isles. As far as I was concerned, there was only one that was any good, and that was the Parachute Regiment. It was a stupid, senseless attitude, really, but the Red Beret really did mean something to those who wore it. It was the same situation as the Marines and dogoes, but instead of calling them dogoes, the British paratrooper referred to all other regiments as 'Land Army' and regarded them as being somewhat inferior.

The North Koreans decided they didn't like the Black Watch after the priest incident, and made good propaganda of it with loudspeakers.

Night after night, almost the same message, like wrath from the heavens, volumed across the valley: 'Black Watch. Black Watch. We know you are there. You know what you have done. And you will pay. Not one of you will leave Korea alive.'

It was eerie, being personalised like that, for, as Leggy pointed out: 'That message goes for us, too, because we are with them.'

'Of course,' said Stan, brightly, 'we could pin notices on our chests saying we are not Black Watch!'

The message was invariably heralded and complemented

by a Chinese woman singing Loch Lomond in an attempted Scottish accent! This infuriated the Jocks more than the message did.

As Einstein might easily have said, all feelings are relative. A Troop will compete with a Troop but the two will combine as a Battery to compete with another Battery, and Batteries will combine as a Regiment to compete with another Regiment, and so on right up to Brigade and Country of Origin level.

That was why I couldn't help feeling rather angry when I heard what the Marines had said to the Black Watch before pulling out: 'The Chinks will have you off The Hook by this time tomorrow.'

No matter that the Black Watch were Land Army – they were British! And they stayed and proved their worth. They dug in much deeper than the Marines had done, and it was the digging-in which reduced their losses considerably.

They were under orders to hold to the last man and the last round when the North Korean Army once again threw its might at The Hook. And so were we.

With bugles blasting and shouts that sounded remarkably like tally-hoes, they came at us like a locust host to the forest. I was convinced on this occasion that they were absolutely suicidal.

And one other thing I noticed. Many of them charged a point without firing and without any thought for the weapons they were carrying.

Leggy and Stan were at either end of the observation slit, firing like mad while I was on the phone, giving orders to the mortars.

'There are three outside here!' Stan yelled, excitedly.

I left the phone just as Leggy and Stan fired, slamming two North Koreans back several yards. I brought my rifle up just as the third reached the observation slit. Then an incredible thing happened.

For that split-second which usually lasts a lifetime, I saw a great gash of grinning teeth in a wooden face. Any other attacking soldier would have thrust his rifle in first, firing at the same time, or flung in a hand grenade. Not this soldier.

126

He held his rifle in one hand, in the carrying position, and he stood there undecided what to do.

Then, still grinning broadly, almost kindly, he reached out his other hand towards my rifle barrel. I squeezed the trigger. And he was gone.

Leggy's command cut through my puzzled thoughts.

'Get the howitzers again,' he said, curtly.

And once more, under Leggy's direction, the howitzers helped to save the day and The Hook. But the battle kept on until dawn. Then the shelling resumed.

When I asked Leggy about the soldier I had shot, he said: 'I think that most of them are drugged up to the eyeballs.'

Peace talks had started up again. Sick and wounded prisoners were being exchanged. But shells were still falling on The Hook.

Then something else fell – North Korean winter, borne to us by the freezing, northern winds from Manchuria.

There's an old joke about the Yukon which claims that the weather is so cold there that anyone having a pee has to break it off the end like a long stick. Winter in North Korea was almost that bad. No one ever lingered when answering Nature's call.

At one stage we were told that the temperature had dropped to −25° Fahrenheit. And fifty-seven degrees of frost is mighty cold. Often, Stan would come in from the cold, shivering and chanting: 'When you're searching for gold, and your balls grow cold and the end of your tool turns blue . . .'

The latrine rail was dispensed with. Backsides would have frozen solid to that. Mucus froze in nostrils, eyelids had the infuriating habit of sticking together and one had to prise them apart with fingers. Parka hoods were rimmed with thick ice by the condensation of breath freezing instantly. The intense cold caused an invisible band of pain, like a vice, to grip one's forehead and eyes. And still we had to keep on fighting.

Getting into the special, white, twin bedding rolls was

127

like sliding between two slabs of ice. Getting out of them in the morning or whenever there was an attack was even worse. Within minutes of pulling the hoods of the bedding rolls closed, icicles hung from them.

Socks had to be changed two or three times a day. Feet will always sweat when encased in thick socks and boots; and quickly the sweat turned to ice, and frostbite would not be long in coming. Washing with iced water was confined to a quick dab on the face and a wet finger drawn across eyebrows, followed by vigorous rubbing with a towel. Shaving was too painful even to contemplate.

Petrol could be poured on to the ground and would not ignite when a match was put to it! No vehicle would start until the carburettor bowl had been taken off and the ice removed. And the ice on the fast-flowing Imjin became so thick that the huge Centurion tanks could be driven across it!

But, thanks to a brilliant soldier, whose name escapes me, we did have respite from the cold. He invented a petrol stove – an upturned petrol can on the roofs of dug-outs and command posts with a narrow pipe running from it into an empty oil drum, fashioned as a stove with a slit for air at the bottom. A regulator tap was inserted in the hose so that the petrol dripped very slowly and ignited as in a Primus stove. And, as far as I can remember, there were never any accidents with this potentially dangerous piece of apparatus.

I often wondered what the rats thought of our being there and all the noise of gunfire. They were everywhere. They would even run, audaciously, along the communication trenches from one dug-out to another. It was obviously worth all the din and blastings to be able to snatch a piece of food now and then and enjoy the warmth of the petrol stoves!

But throughout that harsh winter, morale remained high. When the snow lay deep and crisp and even, I entered the command post on one occasion, greeting everyone with: 'Beautiful weather, isn't it?'

'Yes, deah chap,' replied Charles, 'provided, of course, one is a Yeti!'

Another time, during a lull in a battle, I recited, to Charles's secret delight, the following:

As cold as a frog in an ice-bound pool,
As cold as the hairs round an Eskimo's tool;
As cold as charity – and that's bloody chilly,
But none's so cold as our poor Willie –
Cos he's dead, poor bugger!

'You really are a coarse fellow,' Charles told me. 'But you do have a certain *je ne sais quoi*.'

For entertainment one evening in the command post we managed to piece together all the verses of Macauley's 'How Horatio Kept the Bridge' and I managed to remember all of 'The Burial of Sir John Moore at Corunna'. Many an evening we held poetry sessions with the officers joining in. Blake's tiger burned bright, and Chesterton's donkey had shouts about its ears and palms before its feet. We would go over the hills with Wordsworth or walk the shores of Gitchee Gumee with Hiawatha, or join De la Mare in watching the moon walk the night in a silver shoon. We joined the caravanserai of Omar Khayham, marched with the Pied Piper, laid King Arthur to rest, galloped with the Highwayman and watched the Lady of Shallot crack the mirror. One night we took the message from Aix to Ghent, and hoped that Abu Ben Adam's tribe would increase.

They were good evenings and many times we forgot completely that death stabbed the cold air outside.

On Christmas Day every man turned inwards to his own personal thoughts. Both sides honoured Christ's birthday and fired no shells or bullets on that part of the front.

'At least,' I said, 'we're having a white Christmas. That's more than we usually get back home.'

But my personal Christmas thoughts were troubled. Although I had received regular letters from Mum, Sylvia's had been sparse and short. One part of my mind tried to tell me she was already growing tired of waiting, but I doggedly refused to believe it even though her Christmas card had been perfunctory with just 'Love, Sylvia' and nothing more than the printed greeting, which was applicable to anyone and not especially for a loved-one.

A visiting American padre conducted services in a marquee and, for something to do, I attended with Stan. How different, I thought, from the dreary, mournful dirges in English churches. We sang Negro spirituals to the beat of tambourines, plus a couple of rousing Salvationist hymns.

The padre, too, with sympathetic, crinkled, sparkling eyes, was 'one of the boys' and not the 'holier than thou' type of English parson. Also, he kept his sermon short, the theme of which was the danger of associating with 'diseased' Korean girls! Singing was the more important and happy way of communicating with God. I really enjoyed that service, and left with the sinful thought that some day I should try to find one of those Korean girls!

In keeping with British Army tradition, the officers had served us breakfast in bed, and the cook surpassed himself with turkey and real Christmas plum pudding. During the next couple of days I found myself toying with the idea of telling Bucks folk about the service and Christmas in the front line.

I recalled that when I was thirteen and attending Queen's Park School for Boys in Aylesbury, I had written an essay entitled 'My Brother', telling of Murray's sinkings in the Mediterranean. The headmaster, Mr Jones, had assembled the entire school in the prayer hall and read the essay to them, adding: 'Now, that is how essays should be written.'

I told Charles about my idea of writing an article for the *Bucks Advertiser* and he thought it an excellent one.

'Better let me read it first,' he said, completely devoid of pomposity, 'just in case there are any grammatical errors. Can't have you letting the British Army down.'

I wrote the article under the paraphrased title of a famous book – 'All Quiet on the Christmas Front'. Charles and the officers thought it was very good. I sent it off. To my delight, the then editor, Johnny How, published it without alteration and gave me my first by-line.

Too late to be included in the article – besides which, the front *was* quiet only on Christmas Day – the North

Koreans committed a diabolical and sadistic act on New Year's Eve.

We were back at the F-O-P and Stan and I had made ourselves a snug dug-out in the snow just behind the crest of the hill. It was like a fox's lair, and each night we would pull a slab of rock over the entrance to keep in the warmth, as in an igloo.

On New Year's Eve, I finished watch at midnight, relieved by Jock McEwell, and hurried to the 'igloo' where Stan was already asleep. It was snowing heavily and I was more than glad to get inside and pull the rock to behind me. When the snow stopped at about two thirty in the morning, our igloo was completely covered and hidden.

A North Korean patrol walked right over the top of us – the footsteps were there, plain to see, in the morning. They went on down the hill and across a small valley to where the Turks, brought up close, were sleeping. They cut the throats of twenty Turks, then returned, this time passing by the side of the igloo, in which Stan and I slept peacefully on.

In the morning, when we were told what had happened, the contents of my bowels turned to liquid. Stan fingered his throat and gulped.

Sentries were doubled after that, and two Vickers machine-guns were mounted, ready.

Two nights later, Stan was on watch in the F-O-P and I was asleep on my own in the igloo when the cut-throats came over again.

The Vickers cut them to ribbons and one North Korean left a pool of blood on top of the igloo where he fell. And I slept obliviously on!

'My God!' was all I could say in the morning when Stan told me about it and pointed to the red stain in the snow.

At the end of January, Leggy told us that Commonwealth troops were being withdrawn from the line and we were pulling away from The Hook.

'About time, too,' I said. 'We've been here three stinking months. It's more than time we had a rest.'

'Ah, well, I'm afraid we're not.' Leggy's voice was apologetic. 'Having a rest, that is. We are staying.'

131

'Why?' I exclaimed. 'And who are we going to support? Not the Gooks?'

'No,' said Leggy. 'The Americans.'

'God help us,' said Stan, crossing himself, dramatically.

'Where are we going?' I asked, resignedly.

'Hill Three Five Five.'

Hill Three Five Five is a mountain of almost solid rock. Also known as 'Little Gibraltar', it was bloodily fought for and gained by the King's Own Scottish Borderers. And it was there that a KOSB private called Bill Speakman won the VC.

It was subsequently held, under an onslaught of very heavy fire, by the Australians and the Princess Patricia's Canadian Light Infantry, known as the 'Princess Pat's'. They had the heart of the fighting Turk and the discipline of troops from the British Isles, making them a formidable fighting force.

And now Hill Three Five Five was in the hands of the Americans.

'You'll find the Yanks a queer bunch,' Leggy told us. 'Not at all like the US Marines. Their discipline isn't all it should be, and they seem to have very little sense of self-preservation.'

'How do you mean?' I asked.

'Well, for one thing, they have a funny habit of sitting on skylines. Not conducive to health.'

The F-O-P on Hill Three Five Five was high and wind-swept. It was much more isolated and desolate up there than it was at other F-O-Ps. Because it was on the northern side of the mountain, it had very little of the sun that often shone through the snow clouds, and it had a dark, sinister atmosphere of oppressiveness.

One of the first things I found out up there was that the United States Army marched on its stomach – a sweet and candy one!

I was on my first morning watch when I heard: 'Candies! Cigarettes! Coke! Chewing gum! Tobacco! Matches!'

For a moment, I thought I was hearing things. I went

outside, looked round the corner of a huge rock which jutted and cut off the view to the infantry lines, and there, complete with tray like an icecream girl at the cinema, was an American soldier, walking along the communication trench!

Seemingly oblivious of where he was and the shells that now and then crumped in, this vendor of candies and tobacco was calling on his 'regulars' in their dug-outs just like a milkman or baker on his rounds.

I looked at my wristwatch. It was only ten o'clock. I had never seen anything so incongruous in Korea.

This waitress in Army clothing saw me and came over.

'Need anything, bud?' he asked.

I wished Charles were with me to see and hear this. I looked into the tray. The only thing I could think of for the moment was: 'How often do you come round?'

'Most mornings, if I can make it,' replied the Candy Man.

I bought a packet of Fifth Avenue cigarettes. Now, I had seen everything! What I'd heard about the Americans simply had to be true.

Another American soldier, whose dug-out was the closest to the F-O-P, caught sight of me and called out: 'Hi!'

He sauntered over and introduced himself: 'Call me Manny.'

We shook hands. He was twenty-four, compactly built, with clean-cut features and olive skin. He was slightly Italian looking. He had just bought, among other things, some chewing tobacco.

'Chaw?' he asked, thrusting the plug forward.

'I've never tasted it,' I said. 'What's it like?'

'I like it. Go on – take a piece.'

I put my nose to it first. It smelt sweet and delicious. I took a small bite. Then I spat and spat and spat.

'Ugh! It's fucking revolting!'

Manny laughed. 'You gotta get used to the taste. Like eating tomatoes for the first time.'

He told me he came from Montana and I told him I came from Buckinghamshire. Conversation came easily and time passed quickly. When Stan relieved me at midday, Manny said: 'See you around.'

As the days passed, I couldn't cotton on to the Americans at all. They never seemed to be a close unit. It was as if they were floundering, waiting for guidance. More than an infantry company they resembled a set of individuals who, reluctantly, had been brought together without any apparent reason, in unfortunate circumstances, and were rebelling against it by behaving in a slipshod manner.

I was glad I was in the British Army, which always offered such a nice, comforting cloak of security. It would always look after you, even if it couldn't prevent you from being killed.

I was also glad that I was in the Easy Troop. Even Sergeant-Major Winscombe, with all his faults – in my bigoted and nonconformist eyes – was an intrinsic part of the whole concept of togetherness. There was something intangible about the way the various social classes easily fitted together to fight – even if most of us didn't have a clue what we were fighting for. I reasoned it was always the same with the British when a common enemy was involved.

Then there was that sense of humour always constant in the British Army. On the third day on Hill Three Five Five, I was sent with the jeep to the troop to bring Pretty Boy to the F-O-P for a day's experience. It meant passing through the 'Mad Mile', a length of road enclosed by camouflage netting and constantly under enemy surveillance.

One had a choice – either go like the clappers or brake and dawdle midway and wait for the mortars to explode ahead. There was usually a thirty-second gap between binocular sighting of a vehicle's movement and the fall of mortars. I chose to go like the clappers, winding the speedometer needle round until it stuck on the pin at the bottom.

'If you kill me, Gerald,' exclaimed Pretty Boy, 'I will never speak to you again!'

When we were safely on the other side, the mortars cracking behind us, Pretty Boy asked me: 'Where *did* you learn to drive?'

'In Germany,' I said. 'Don't tell anyone, but I never actually *passed* a driving test.'

'What?' he exclaimed. 'My God! And I'll always remember that night in the ammunition truck! How did you manage to get driver/operator entered in your pay-book?'

I grinned. 'The specialist mortar battery that I joined in Germany, after I had been kicked out of the Paras, had only just been formed. A new assignment of three-ton trucks had arrived at Hanover and all drivers were asked to put up their hands.'

'And you put your hand up, no doubt.'

'Of course! My father drove the first car in Whitchurch and put me behind the wheel of an old Canadian Buick that we used to pull the hay and dung carts when I was only eight. And I drove tractors after I started working, and there were the cars I borrowed to get back to camp when the last bus had gone. But a three-tonner is huge and it was pretty frightening at first, but I managed to get it back to barracks in one piece, though I did knock an old lady off her bike when I didn't give her a wide enough berth on a bend. I got a severe reprimand for that.

'Allowing enough space for the back wheels to get through on a turn or bend was always my problem. I was always mounting the kerb and once when we were camping in a forest I left a trail of flattened trees as I wove in and out of them. So long as I got my cab through, it was sod the back.

'But the only real accident I ever had was when we were on manoeuvres. I was tearing down a narrow country lane near Flensburg with a chap called Bullock in the passenger seat. Rounding a bend we came face-to-face with a dirty big Sheridan tank that also wasn't exactly hanging about. Its sharp-angled corner above the track sliced through the bottom of the cab on Bullock's side like a knife through butter. I can still see his face. He gave a sort of strangled "Eeeee! Ooooh" but had the presence of mind to lift his legs high and the corner of the tank slid under him, pushing his seat slightly higher before both vehicles came to a stop after the truck had been thrust back several yards.

'After that I had a reputation of being a maniac driver. One day my truck and another one were parked, waiting to take a swimming party to the local baths. Everyone climbed

135

into the back of my one. "Who's driving?" someone asked. "I am," I declared. "Oh, my Christ! It's Kingy!" shouted someone else, and they all leapt out. And no matter how much the subaltern tried to persuade them, they wouldn't get back in. After that it was decided that my truck should only be used for inanimate goods.'

Laughing, Pretty Boy asked: 'But who wrote driver/operator in your pay-book?'

'Bullock,' I replied. 'Not only was he my pal, he was a driving instructor!' And that left Pretty Boy speechless.

12

'These bloody Yanks seem to do nothing but loll about all day, incessantly chewing!' I grumbled to Stan.

'Don't their jaws ever ache?' he asked me.

There was definitely something lacking where the Americans, as a fighting unit, were concerned but it was an impalpable thing. However, towards the end of the first week I did get a glimpse through to the root of the problem when I was on my way round to the F-O-P.

A young lieutenant was reprimanding a soldier for not cleaning his rifle. The soldier didn't even rise to his feet. He just lay on his bedding-roll in his dug-out and told the officer to 'Fuck off!'

And the flustered and frustrated young lieutenant did just that without saying another word.

I had taken a liking to Manny and he to me. I told him about the incident and asked him why the Americans were like they were.

He laughed. 'For one thing,' he said, 'we aren't fighters like you Britishers. We're lovers!'

I felt a bit embarrassed at that. Speaking for myself, I knew I'd rather have sex than fight at any time. The Americans, too, had a reputation where women were concerned. But 'lovers'! I had never heard that euphemism before.

'I always thought that the French were supposed to be the lovers in this world. Not the Americans. Because of the films that Hollywood churns out, we regard you guys as tough he-men with guns on your hips. Just look how Errol Flynn captured Burma and you Yanks never even saw the skies over the place!'

'Hollywood is crap,' replied Manny. 'You guys just don't know us at all. We don't want to fight. None of us like fighting. Most of us are kids and don't want to be out here. We've got our own lives to lead. If half of us had the guts we'd be registered conscientious objectors. We've just been dragged into the Army and made to come out here.'

'We have conscription, too,' I told him, 'but at least our chaps do have a try at being soldiers.'

'Like I said, it's because you're born fighters,' he replied. 'You a Regular soldier?'

I nodded.

'Thought perhaps you were.'

The next night, and the next, all of us on Hill Three Five Five were entertained by 'fireworks' on Pork Chop Hill in the American sector proper. It was too far to hear the mortar and gunfire; like watching a silent movie except when the real heavy shells crumped in. For the two nights it was almost daylight there. There seemed to be no break in the flashes.

'Pork Chop is definitely being fried,' I said to Stan, as we stood, watching. 'And it's pretty weird when you think about it, for there's us here, safe, and those poor bastards over there getting blown to bits. Yet we are all part of the same war.'

'I suppose it's all a matter of luck which hill you happen to be on,' he said.

Three nights later we happened to be out of luck. We were on Hill Three Five Five!

A South Korean and I were filling sandbags when the first mortar crept in without warning. The South Korean's legs suddenly gave way and he lay on his back, face upwards. He had two mouths, the larger one being a gash where his eyes had been. I was splattered with blood and minced flesh and bone.

'Christ!' I yelled, my ears pounding from the explosion. Earth poured from a long slit in the filled sandbag I was lifting to stack. The sandbag had saved me.

Then mortars were falling like a cloudburst. I grabbed my rifle and ran to the safety of the observation post, which was hewn from the rock itself. Stan was inside, tuning the main wireless set to the guns.

'Where's Leggy?' I asked, as I dashed in. 'It's bloody murder out there. Splintered rock is flying as thick as the shrapnel.'

'He's gone round to the F-O-P to see Jock. It sounds bloody awful enough in here.'

I snatched up the field telephone. 'Jock? The Gook's just been killed. Tell Leggy.'

Leggy came on to the phone. 'Bad about the Gook,' he said. 'You all right?'

'Just about.'

'Good. This is probably going to be a long and nasty one like Pork Chop received. Tell McCleod to see that every radio battery is fully charged, and you check on water and rations.'

'Right!' I said.

The mortars kept coming in until midnight. Then their place was taken by heavy shells at varying intervals. At eight o'clock the next morning, the mortars started again.

We lost Jock McEwell shortly afterwards as he was about to dash to the F-O-P to relieve me. The blast blew him backwards into the observation post. He died as Leggy gave him a morphine injection.

I stayed on in the F-O-P to do Jock's watch. By the time Stan relieved me at two o'clock in the afternoon, I was, in my own words, 'knackered'. I was allowed to sleep until eight o'clock – a good six hours. Stan woke me. He told me that McCleod had returned with more batteries and another wireless set.

'We've had word there's going to be a big attack tonight,' he added.

The fall of shells was regular and deafening. Heavy atmospherics were coming through on the radio. Leggy outlined the procedure. The four of us – the only Britishers on Hill Three Five Five at the time – would stay in the observation post until dusk. Then he and I would stand watch in the F-O-P while Stan and Jock would attend to the observation post.

As usual, there were three remote-control lines to the F-O-P and we would operate the set from there. Dug in very very deeply was a telephone in case of emergency.

'We'll have a Browning manned just by our right, and just behind us to the left there'll be a Vickers,' said Leggy. 'The Americans will be in three lines – one in front of us and two behind. That sniper chappie, Manny, or whatever he's called, will be with us in the F-O-P.'

Digging-in on Three Five Five had meant pick-axe, sledge-hammer and crowbar. Each unit that manned Three Five Five made it just that little bit more habitable for the next. By now the dug-outs were deeply cut into the side and protected by sandbagged entrances.

The sun dipped behind us to the left. 'Right!' said Leggy, and he and I ran the gauntlet of exploding shells to the F-O-P. We arrived unscathed but breathless with fright and effort, and found Manny looking through the 'donkey's ears'.

'Can't see a darned thing any more,' he said.

'I don't expect you can,' replied Leggy, drily. 'There'll be a moon tonight, though.'

'Any idea what time this attack is expected?' Manny asked.

'We have it as about o-two hundred hours.'

'That's an awfully long nerve-racking time to wait, listening to these shells,' Manny commented.

'Cheer up,' I said. 'The attack may come before that.'

But Intelligence wasn't far wrong. The attack came at two thirty when the moon was skipping in and out of the clouds. We had been taking turns to doze and I awoke suddenly to the familiar blasts of bugles. Then small arms joined the thunder of shellfire.

Because of the mountain's height there was nothing much we could do with our big guns under close attack. The trajectories were too low. Even if the shells were made to skim the top they would still go too far and over the heads of the advancing North Koreans. Mortars and small arms were our only hope, and Leggy kept the former hard at it. We were told later that water was poured down the barrels to stop them becoming red-hot. And so was beer!

It was comforting to know that we had a machine-gun on either side of us. When the Browning stopped Leggy dashed along to see what was wrong.

He came puffing back and told me: 'They're changing

belts. But the two Americans manning the gun are shitting cubic yards. This could be very, very nasty.'

Then he emptied his revolver through the observation slit. He had just finished reloading, and his finger was curled lovingly round the trigger, when the telephone rang. He kept his forefinger round the trigger and pressed his middle finger to one ear, the .38 pointing dangerously into his woollen cap-comforter. He pressed the receiver hard against his other ear.

'I see,' he said, when Stan had finished speaking. 'Tell them message understood. Wilco.'

He put the phone down and motioned me to join him. Manny was busy, cracking away with his carbine.

'That was a directive from Tactical Headquarters,' he told me in a loud whisper. 'Should the Yanks break and run under this lot, our orders are to stay, directing shellfire at all costs. You know what that means, don't you?'

'Yes,' I said, simply.

'Good lad. I know I can depend on you, McCleod and Sutton.'

'Yes,' I said again.

But as Stan said to me later, almost echoing my thoughts: 'When I heard that message that maybe the four of us would be left alone to face that screaming, maniacal lot out there, I thought it was so hysterically funny it was enough to give you the shits for a fortnight!'

'Christ! They're everywhere!' Manny suddenly yelled.

Leggy and I leapt to the observation slit. They were, too! The North Koreans seemed to be in every communication trench, running hither and thither and dying like flies.

'Tell the mortars to drop fifty!' Leggy yelled to me. 'Yes, I know it's close, but we'll all have to take that chance.'

'Christ!' said Manny, again. 'This carbine's gonna seize up soon.'

'Have a go with this,' I said, handing him my .303. 'I have to contact the mortars.'

Leggy's decision to drop the mortars by fifty yards really paid off. The eight bombs crumped in right where the largest mass of North Koreans had gathered, halfway up the forward slope, obliterating most of them. The next eight bombs fell almost immediately, followed by the next eight and the next almost on top of each other.

Once again Leggy used his favourite adjective: 'Beautiful! Beautiful!'

I picked up Manny's carbine. 'How does this thing work?' I shouted.

'Just keep pulling the trigger!' he yelled back.

The .30 carbine had a vee sight. I liked that much better than the .303's peep-hole sight. But really, the North Koreans were so thick out there, I didn't need any sights at all. None the less, I picked myself a North Korean who seemed to have lost his balance on top of a communication trench bank. His arms were flailing when I fired.

I didn't know where the shot went. Certainly not into the North Korean. Two Americans quickly blasted him to eternity before I could get a second shot.

'The sights are too high for that range,' Manny yelled. 'You went above him.'

We exchanged rifles. For about three hours the North Koreans came in waves of attack. Leggy's mortar direction made sure that a few hundred of them would never attack anything else. Then the North Koreans had had enough. The last lot were going back. Leggy was waiting with the 25-pounders. He was more than satisfied as the creeping barrage took its toll.

'OK,' said Leggy, when all was quiet except for the occasional shot. 'That's it. I'll send Sutton round with some beer.'

'Where's he going?' asked Manny, when Leggy had gone.

'Round to your command post for a whisky, I expect,' I replied.

I lit a cigarette and Manny cut off a piece of tobacco and began chewing.

'Well,' I commented, 'for a self-confessed, non-aggressive lover, you're a pretty good fighter!'

He grinned. 'Just the laws of self-preservation,' he said. 'How'd you like the carbine?'

'All right. But it doesn't feel as solid as the .303.'

142

Manny nodded. 'I thought the .303 a mite heavy. But she's a great gun.'

Anyone in the British Army who was heard calling a rifle a gun was usually made to stand on the parade ground, rifle in one hand and penis in the other, and recite

> This is my rifle,
> This is my gun;
> This is to fight with,
> This is for fun!

But I let the discrepancy go. 'It was quite a night, wasn't it?' I asked.

Manny nodded again. 'Sure was.' He spat a black-looking stream through the observation slit. 'Those bastards sure know how to die.'

'They're probably pumped full of Benzedrine,' I told him.

He laughed. 'Yeah. They get the Bennies and we get the bromide!'

'I think I'm going to see if I can have some more R-and-R,' I went on.

'I only came back a month ago,' he said. 'You've been before, then? Those Japanese chicks are really something. How many did you lay?'

'Five,' I said. I refrained from mentioning what had occurred, subsequently!

'Not bad! Not bad at all!' He thought for a moment. 'So you ain't a family man. Or are you?'

'Christ, no. My round shoulders are just natural! I probably will be, though, when I get back. *If* I get back. But I think she's forgotten about me,' I went on, wistfully. 'I haven't heard from her since Christmas.'

'I shouldn't worry,' he comforted me. 'The mail's been haywire lately.'

I was telling him about Sylvia when Stan arrived. He had three bottles clutched to his chest and one in his hand. He looked around the F-O-P.

'Been a battle round here?' he asked, casually.

'Never mind the wisecracks, let's have the beer,' I said, reaching for a bottle.

Stan handed a bottle to Manny and put the other two on the floor.

'Talk has it,' he told us, 'that there won't be any more fighting tonight.' He went back to the observation post.

'My old man's a general,' Manny suddenly said. 'Can you beat that?'

'In that case, I should have thought the Army was a natural career for you.'

'Yeah.' Bitterly. 'But I don't want it. It's a hell of a thing to live up to. And my old man's so righteous and God-fearing, it hurts. And my sister is getting to be like him. Christ, man, if they knew how I really lived, I guess they'd die of shock. Drink and women are strictly taboo at home. No bad language, nothing.'

'My mother's fairly easy going,' I said. 'In fact, if anything, she's a bit earthy. We had a lodger during the war, and I'm sure he fancied my mother. He was always more than eager to do things for her. One Christmas, when we were sitting round the fire, with a bunch of holly hanging above the mantelpiece, a hot coal dropped out. He jumped up to put it back on the fire and let out two walloping big farts. By the sheerest of coincidences, two holly leaves fluttered down. "Got 'em!" shouted Mum; and he left the room very red-faced!'

Manny laughed and I laughed with him. 'You're lucky, real lucky,' he said. 'I don't know if my old man ever had any good times. If he did, he's forgotten all about them. When I'm home I have to act like the All-American Boy again. They must think the Army believes in celibacy. It's purgatory. Purgatory. Do you know . . .' He stopped.

'Do I know what?' I asked.

'Nothing. It doesn't matter.'

There was silence for a while, save for the gurgle of beer going down. I broke the silence.

'How old's your sister?'

'Eighteen.'

'Doesn't she go out with boys?'

Manny snorted. 'She's the bee's knees of virtue. If a man grabbed her ass, she'd faint clean away. And not with

144

ecstasy, either. I had a few furloughs before I came out here and I always lied about them. I always halved the amount of time I had on my pass. You know the kinda thing. It's like being smothered when I'm home. I was pampered as a child and never wanted for nothing.'

I told him I did the same with my leaves to be with Sylvia, and I asked about his mother.

'Dead,' he replied, succinctly.

'My father's dead, too,' I said, and we let it go at that.

'What was your childhood like?' he wanted to know.

'Idyllic. We weren't rich and we weren't poor. But I had everything that I wanted – open fields and farm animals. I didn't care about anything else. Do you know, I was ten years old before I put down an electric light switch.'

'Primitive, eh?' he said, just as the field telephone rang.

It was Stan, announcing firmly that he was 'going to kip'.

'Yes, but I never noticed the primitiveness,' I said, putting the phone down. 'I was blissfully happy. Then war came along and spoilt everything. We were forced to leave the village and move into the near-by town. Aylesbury, it's called.'

Music, similar to Country and Western, came floating, faintly, from across the valley.

'Chinky's up to his usual pranks,' I said.

'What forced you to leave?' Manny asked.

'My father was a liveried chauffeur for a Scottish laird who had moved south and bought this thousand-acre estate.

'The laird died, just before I was born in a wooden bungalow next to the estate's farm. Lady Duthie, his widow, managed the affairs until war broke out. She decided that Scotland might be healthier with all the bombs dropping around us, sold up and told my father to get lost. We had to move to the town for him to find work. As you can imagine, I don't have much time for Britain's aristocracy.'

'But what was it like, living in a village?' Manny prompted me. 'We only hear stories of English towns.'

'A different, more down-to-earth attitude altogether. Some townfolk call country folk "rustics", "yokels" and "sheep-shaggers".'

145

I had to explain the meaning of the last word, and he chuckled. 'Just like our hill-billies back home. Wellington boots and all?'

'Too true! It's the standard joke. All rustics shag sheep. Of course, I'm a bit out of touch with village life now, but I remember a bad thing about it – everybody knew everything about everybody. There were no secrets. I don't know what Whitchurch – the name of the village – is like now, but when I was born in 1930 superstition was rife. Witches still flew on broomsticks and headless ghosts walked the candle-lit corridors. And the church and chapel seemed to support those weird beliefs and they ruled with a mighty hand. Almost everything outside of breathing was Sin, with a capital S, and we even had to thank God for breath!

'We had only a crystal radio that jerked and squawked out music and voices, and our His Master's Voice gramophone – complete with huge megaphone – did little for Jack Buchanan's "Goodnight, Vienna"!

'Telling stories – the same ones over and over again – was the main entertainment in living rooms, lit only by paraffin lamps. Much better than listening to a banshee striving for a top note while another member of the family accompanied her on an anything but tuneful piano.'

'I know,' said Manny. 'We had those awful musical evenings, too. But my mother did have a good voice, and our grand piano was always kept in tune.'

We each opened a second bottle of beer. As if on cue, the record was changed on the other side of the valley.

'That's original for those bastards,' commented Manny. 'Chinky must like us!'

'To give you an idea of the mentality of Whitchurch people when I was a boy,' I continued, 'I'll tell you an oft-told story, if you like.'

'Why not?' responded Manny. 'There's nothing else to do. And we ain't going anywhere.'

So, while medics continued collecting the dead and attending the wounded, and ambulance helicopters whirled in and out, I told him about 'Black-headed Nan'.

It was a story that, whenever I heard it as a little boy,

146

always filled me with awe and dread. Many times throughout my telling of it, in a bullet-and-shrapnel-scarred F-O-P, thousands of miles from Whitchurch, Manny exclaimed and commented.

Black-headed Nan was a dignified Gypsy woman who arrived in Whitchurch one day and used to sell very cheap wooden clothes-pegs on Sunday afternoons. After a month, however, the villagers grew tired of having their Sunday afternoon naps disturbed and a highly religious woman called Massive Ada took it upon herself to protect them.

The following Sunday she was waiting for the knock and yanked open the front door when it came. Her stentorian boom filled the road: 'You wicked woman! May God strike you down for selling your wares on His day. Bugger off, you heathen! Go on, bugger off, I say!'

And Ada slammed the door shut.

People who heard it said Black-headed Nan's howl of rage was worse than a vixen's call to its mate and that she screeched out a terrible curse on Ada's house.

The next morning Ada's husband, Tom, the church warden, walked down the back garden to the lavatory, as usual, and when he had seated himself comfortably pitched forward stone dead!

Well, naturally everyone took fright when they heard the news and the following Sunday all the doors were locked and bolted. But the door of one very poor family wasn't locked. When the black figure knocked, it was instantly opened and a gruesome head popped out. Five-year-old Nancy's scalp, forehead and ears were encrusted with hard, cracked and bleeding scabs of ringworm.

Nancy's mother rushed to shut the door but Black-headed Nan hissed that she could cure the child. The following morning, the mother was to collect as many large black slugs as she could find. She should stab them with a long darning needle until all the slimy juice was drained and smear that over the child's head. Then she should put on a thick bandage and not touch it again until Black-headed Nan returned.

Frightened out of her wits, the mother did as she was

told. The following Sunday afternoon, when Black-headed Nan took off the bandage Nancy's head was as clean as a whistle. All the dried scabs came away with the bandage and her hair had started to grow.

When I finished telling the story, Manny and I discussed whether Tom's sudden death and the cure of the ringworm were solely coincidence. Our verdict on the story was that Black-headed Nan had acquitted herself well and that Ada had not behaved as a Christian!

13

The following day, I was told that I couldn't go on R-and-R again for at least a month.

'Four more rotten weeks to go until I can get a lay,' I complained to Manny.

'Tough,' was the laconic reply. Then, smiling, he said: 'I really enjoyed last night. You should write those stories. You'd make people laugh. Laughter's important in this lousy world.'

Manny seemed to spend most of his time in the F-O-P. At least, he always happened along when I was there. I really enjoyed his company and told him more stories about Whitchurch. My hours on watch went much faster than if I had been on my own. I missed him during the spates that Dog Troop relieved us.

The four weeks gradually passed. There were one or two small skirmishes at night-time. The harassing shells crunched in during the day, and the Americans kept dying in ones and twos. I thought them as good as any Marine, and told Manny so.

To this day, I don't know what happened to the North Koreans who fell on our ground. Always, in the morning after a battle, the bodies had gone. But on a mound just in front and to the right of the F-O-P was the rotting body of a North Korean. For some reason, nobody bothered to collect it. Stan and I would often use the body for target practice when there was nothing much else to do. It was a realistic target. Every time a bullet hit it, a piece would fly off!

Looking at the body, early one morning after entering the F-O-P, Manny said: 'If I had to leave my rotting carcase behind in this God-forsaken land, I reckon I'd die of shame!'

He squinted along the sights at the dead North Korean and squeezed the trigger. And yet another piece left the sadly depleted body.

'Spot on this morning,' he said, and applied the safety catch.

'I'm happy,' he continued. 'I gotta letter last night.'

Seeing the sadness in my face at the remark, he said: 'Gee! I'm sorry. Still haven't heard?'

I shook my head. 'Still,' I said, bravely, 'one more night to go, and it's Tokyo for me.'

'Don't rub it in,' he replied, and was silent for a while. Then: 'I've never told you about Sadie, have I?'

'No. Who's she?'

'The most gorgeous creature that ever lived. My girl back home.'

'Never knew you had one.'

He grinned. 'Nobody does. I've never told anyone about her.'

'Why not? And why tell me?'

'Oh, I don't know. I like you. I can talk to you more than I can to anybody else in the outfit.'

'Thanks,' I said, feeling a little embarrassed. 'What's the trouble?'

'First off, I met her in the Bronx,' he said; which at that time meant nothing to me. 'But she's really something.'

'Going to marry her?' I asked.

'She wanted us to get married on my embarkation leave, but I couldn't go through with it. I told her it would be something for us to look forward to when I got back. I bought her the biggest rock I could find. It took me three months to catch up on my pay.'

'Well, I hope she's worth it,' I replied. 'What do your father and sister say about her?'

'That's the trouble. I can't tell them about her.'

'Why? She got leprosy or something?'

Manny shook his head in exasperation. 'Don't you understand? She's from the Bronx. The other side of the tracks.'

'Well,' I said, surprised. 'I didn't know you Yanks had class distinction. I thought only the British had that.'

'I'll say we have! And on top of her being from the Bronx, she's a dancer.'

'Nothing wrong with that,' I told him. 'Many of our gracious duchesses were chorus girls.'

'I know, but Sadie takes her clothes off as she dances!'

'A stripper!' I exclaimed, with more interest in my voice. 'Got a photo of her?'

Manny produced one from his wallet.

'Wow!' was my response when I saw it. 'Haven't you asked her to keep you supplied with more like this?'

Manny laughed. 'Sure,' he said. 'But the others are private, like.'

The photo was of a well-endowed blonde, wearing a provocative smile and little else. 'Yes,' I said, 'I can see the problem.'

'Can you imagine the introduction?' Manny asked. '"I want you to meet Sadie. She does a strip in a club every night."'

'But why tell them? She's a beautiful girl and I'm sure she looks really good in clothes.'

'They'd find out. She was born on the wrong side of the tracks and she had it pretty rough. As soon as she opened her mouth, they'd know.'

'Well, for your sake, I hope she's got something more than sex.'

'What are you saying? Sex is only part of our relationship. She's warm, loving and understanding and – hell, you know what I mean.'

'I wish you all the luck in the world,' I said.

'Oh, I expect Sadie and I will manage OK. If it comes to a break between my father and sister and me – well, that's how it will have to be.'

'If I were you,' I told him, 'I'd write to your father and tell him about her. You'd probably find he'd be very understanding – especially after doing your bit out here. Just let him and your sister see that Sadie's the one for you. If they've really got any love for you, they'll accept her.'

Manny didn't answer for a while. 'Yeah, well I've got to do something. I've been thinking about it until it has almost driven me crazy. It's a kinda relief to have told it to you.'

Manny's face took on a broad smile. 'If only you could meet Sadie. She's, well, she's – just right!'

Stan came rushing into the F-O-P to relieve me. He was all excited.

'Guess what?' he said. 'Leggy says I can go on R-and-R with you!'

'That's marvellous,' I said.

Manny looked at me. 'I reckon there'll be a letter waiting for you from Sylvia when you get back, so don't be too unfaithful to her!' He shook my hand hard. 'Have a nice time,' he said. 'And I appreciate what you said.'

14

We didn't arrive at Camp Ebisu until after one o'clock in the morning, and although the old excitement of the anticipated hunt was there, I felt too tired to hit the town. Stan was the same, so we went to the NAAFI and had fried egg, chips and beans, washed down with a couple of beers. Then we went to our beds, stretching ourselves luxuriously between clean, linen sheets.

It was while we were in the NAAFI that Stan encouraged me: 'Cheer up, Kingy. I thought you once told me that Sylvia was getting fed up with her job and was hoping to move to London in the New Year. She's probably waiting until she gets fixed up before writing.'

'Yes, I know. I've been clinging to that hope.'

In the morning we decided it was best to send presents home straight away before we spent all our money on pleasure. Through a postal service run by the Women's Voluntary Service I sent Mum a beautifully hand-painted six-piece Japanese tea-set, made of wafer-thin bone china. For Sylvia I selected and paid for an ornate Japanese fan, but told the WVS woman that I didn't know the address, and to hold the fan for me until I sent the address from Korea.

For some reason I didn't feel like sending the fan until I received a letter from Sylvia; besides which, if she had moved I didn't know the new address.

Stan wrote a couple of letters and I wrote to Mum. Then, after lunch in camp, we grabbed a taxi.

But Sylvia persisted in my thoughts that first night, and nothing I encountered really appealed, though Stan got himself fixed up with a trim-waisted, pert little thing. I went back to camp and Stan arrived at eleven o'clock in the morning. We had agreed that if we got separated we would always meet back at camp at eleven.

It was on the second night, in a bar, that I met Hirono. She was a Japanese version of Lena Horne and was as hot as Hades. She wore a scarlet, silk blouse, matching high-heeled shoes and a tight black skirt.

After seeing a couple of sexy films to put us in the right frame of mind, Stan and I had gone into the bar for a pre-girl-search John Collins. The bar just happened to be first-class for girls.

Hirono was talking to two girls as we walked in. She looked up, met my eyes and read the message in them. She said something to her friends, who laughed, and walked sensuously over to us. Her body, with its small, thrusting breasts, was almost touching mine when she stopped.

'How would you like to fuck me?' she asked, huskily.

'How subtle,' said Stan. 'She'll probably give you a dose, Kingy.'

Her eyes gave Stan a cold look, dismissing him.

'I bet you got red hair down there,' she went on, and she touched me with expert fingers.

I decided to be coy. 'Wouldn't you like to know?' I said.

She really excited me and, ignoring Stan's warnings, I left him to 'find your own woman' and went off, arm-in-arm with Hirono. She took me to a hotel where she dispensed with customary bathings.

As soon as I closed the door, she came at me, all animal, and glued her lips to mine. I dropped my hands to the hem of her skirt and drew it up to her waist. It was so tight that it stayed there. I dropped my hands once more and felt her soft, stockinged thighs. I thrilled as I caressed their gossamer sheerness. I ran my fingers all over their smoothness from her knees to their tops where I encountered the satin warmth of her skin. I played with the suspender clasps, hooked my fingers behind their black, lacy straps and drew my hands up to her scarlet knickers.

As my fingers tickled their way into her groin, she became a wild thing. She bit me and clutched my hair.

'Your beautiful red hair,' she moaned.

154

I let my hands run over the silky material of her knickers. As my hands went to their elasticated waist and began to pull them down, her hands were feverishly undoing my belt and buttons.

We pulled apart from each other. She to remove her knickers. I to take off my trousers and underpants. Hirono was an artist at removing her knickers. She did it quickly yet sensuously. I watched as she lifted one leg, then the other, the knickers making a swishing sound as each gossamer-clad leg removed itself from them. The sapling was at bursting point.

She stood, breathing heavily, her skirt still up around her waist, the suspender straps on her swelling thighs like parallel guide lines to the black triangle of hair. I went to her and the sapling rubbed her smooth belly. She squirmed her hips. I pressed myself harder against her. Then she overbalanced as the insides of her knees touched the bed, and she fell backwards.

She twisted to stop herself falling, and I fell on top of her. I found myself attacking her from the rear, and at a different place!

'Oh! Oh!' she moaned, softly. 'No. Not there.' Her voice was languid, not commanding. I began pushing. Something gave a little.

'Oh, no,' she cried, but it was more a groan of pleasure. She relaxed, then suddenly thrust herself up to meet and encompass me.

My orgasm was soon upon me. And so was hers with what my hands were doing beneath her. She bit the quilt and drummed the toes of her shoes on the floor.

We lay there, still and quiet for several seconds. Then we rolled over on to our backs. I sat up and took cigarettes and matches from my tunic pocket.

'No one has ever done that to me before,' she said, accepting the lighted cigarette.

'First time I've ever done it,' I replied, the thought occurring that Tokyo must now, surely, have made my education, sex-wise, complete.

We arose and went to the bathroom. Clean, satiated

and tired we went to bed naked and slept in each other's arms.

Next morning, she was fully dressed when she awakened me.

'What you wanna do?' she asked, nibbling the lobe of my ear.

'Huh?' I mumbled.

'What you wanna do? Stay with me another night? I show you Tokyo. Be your wife.'

My eyes focused, and my hand went straight up her skirt. She allowed it to stay there and caress her through the silk knickers.

'Come back to bed,' I urged.

She stood up, away from my hand, and went to the window.

'Look,' she said, sweeping her arm to the sunshine streaming in, 'it is very late. And I am hungry. Let us take breakfast. It much better if we make love again tonight. Better to wait for it. Please? OK?' She smiled. I smiled back.

Obviously a professional, I thought. She wanted to keep me eager for another night. No morning love for me. She could lose money that way. Already she had cost me four thousand yen – two and a half thousand for her, fifteen hundred for the room. Plus drinks, of course. But she was very attractive and fun to be with.

'OK,' I said, and got out of bed.

She was full of Eastern Promise and told me over breakfast how exciting it was to savour throughout the day what we were going to do that night.

She took me to the Ginza Mart, Tokyo's famous market place, and it was there that I bought the first pornographic book I had ever seen. Called the *Autobiography of a Flea*, it related the many amorous adventures of a Victorian lady as seen through the eyes of a flea who lived in her pubic hairs.

The book certainly went the rounds of the Korean battery of mortars when I took it back with me. Charles's comment after reading was: 'Quite an inventive story, and has high literary merit.'

As Hirono guided me on through the market place, she

told me: 'Japanese women have one aim in life – to please their men. You have much money?'

'A little,' I said. 'Why?'

'OK. You buy sexy underwear. I wear for you tonight.'

I went wild at the lingerie stall. With Hirono's feminine understanding of a true sex maniac with a silk and stocking fetish to guide me, I bought a pair of skin-pink French knickers with wide lacy legs, black nylon stockings, a red suspender belt and bra, and a cream and blue full-length petticoat.

The uninitiated might have called the colour scheme revolting, but I was ecstatic. So was Hirono. She clutched the brown paper parcel to her, joyously.

After lunch at a typical Japanese café-restaurant, we went to the theatre. I didn't understand much of it, but it was highly erotic and full of nude women. Hirono laughed quite a lot.

Sensing how the play was affecting me, she undid my trouser buttons and inserted her hand. She raised her buttock, the better to accommodate my hand, and there we sat with innocence on our faces and lust in our loins until the play ended.

It was dark when we came out. We had a couple of drinks in a bar, then walked along the bright, gaily lit street. It was nice having a woman like Hirono on my arm. Many Japanese stopped and turned to look at us.

'There is a hotel I would like to stay at,' she said, 'but we have to travel on the Underground train.'

It was rush hour and we were swept into the carriage and packed like sardines. The stench of sweat, garlic and hair lacquer filled me with nausea; then, thankfully, it was our stop and we breathed fresh air again. We dined, then booked into the hotel, which was clean and inexpensive.

Hirono let me bath first. I came out of the bathroom naked.

'Red hair down there really excites me,' she said.

Before I could take advantage of such an opening remark, she had picked up her brown paper parcel, entered the bathroom and closed the door behind her.

I rang for room service. I was lying on the bed, sipping a John Collins and reading what the flea had written, when she came back.

She was shimmering gossamer from her shoulders to her toes. She looked radiantly, silkenly sensual. The petticoat hugged her, accentuating her hips. She swished with every step. She swished as she sat on the bed to sip her drink. She swished as, keeping her feet on the floor, she let her body sink back on to the bed, the petticoat riding up to reveal the black nylon stockings moulding her luxurious and inviting thighs.

I took her almost drained glass and put it with mine on the bedside table. Then I knelt on the carpet between her long, shapely legs and, remembering what the Eurasian had taught me, I lowered my head. She lay still, then jumped and lay still again.

After a minute she began, very slowly at first, to gyrate her hips. I looked up along her belly and over her bosom and saw that her eyes were closed and her mouth was open. I lowered my head again. Her hips worked faster. Then she clutched my shoulders with both hands.

'Quickly!' she gasped. 'I must have you inside me!'

'Oh, it's lovely!' she cried. 'Lovely!'

We wriggled to a more comfortable position on the bed and fell asleep. We awoke a few hours later and made love again. Then she undressed and we got into bed and slept until mid-morning.

I stayed with her for yet another day and night. Then, suddenly, it was all over between us. We both wanted to go off to pastures new.

It was a tacit understanding. We never even said goodbye. I just got out of bed in the morning, dressed while she watched, silently, and then I left.

I got back to Camp Ebisu in time to catch lunch, and found Stan halfway through his.

'You dirty stop-out,' he greeted me.

'She was worth every penny I spent on her,' I told him.

'Where is she now?'

'I ditched her. Had enough of her.'

158

'If ever I saw a dose of clap walking on two legs, that was her,' said Stan.

'Jealousy will get you nowhere,' I retorted.

'You're a bloody fine one for company on leave,' he complained. 'I haven't seen anything of you.'

'Yes, well, you know how it is. You manage OK?'

Stan tried to look mysterious. 'Can't grumble,' he said, aloofly. Then he grinned. 'As a matter of fact, I've only just got here, myself. After you left with dose of clap I found a gorgeous girl in a small hotel not far from the bar. And I've been with her till now.'

We compared notes and I found that he, too, had been to the Ginza Mart and to the same erotic theatre, but at different times.

In the afternoon we went down town again. And we met the first broke American we'd ever seen. He was trying to walk along the street, almost legless, and he told us he had no money left to get back to Camp Drake, where the Americans were based in Tokyo.

'I got this bottle of Bourbon here,' he slurred. 'Gimme five hundred yen and it's yours.'

'OK,' I said, 'but I think you'd better go to a café first and have some coffee.'

The American's eyes tried to focus but failed. He raised his arms, despairingly. Stan and I grabbed him and half-carried him to a near-by café. We sat him at a table, gave him the five hundred yen, took his bottle and ordered coffee.

The American took a couple of sips then lurched to his feet. 'I gotta piss and be sick,' he groaned.

We guided him to the lavatory and went back to the table.

'Let's open the bottle and have it with our coffee,' suggested Stan.

We sat there, drinking the pleasing mixture and forgot all about the American for about fifteen minutes.

'Where is the bastard?' I growled, suddenly remembering. 'Better go see, I suppose.'

We found him lying half-length on the lavatory floor with his head in a half-full urinal. He was out cold but still breathing.

'Christ!' exclaimed Stan. 'It's a wonder he hasn't drowned in the piss and sick.'

We lifted him up. 'Phew! He stinks!' I said.

We carried him out through the café and laid him on the pavement. Then we hailed a taxi.

'Camp Drake,' I said, when we'd put the American into the back. 'He'll pay when you get there.'

The driver nodded, all grin and teeth. 'Camp Drake. Camp Drake. OK. OK. Me understand,' he said, and went off with a screech of tyres.

Feeling like Good Samaritans, we went back to the café and the bottle of Bourbon. The gold-toothed waitress smiled at us.

'You want jig-a-jig?' she asked.

'Go away, you slagheap,' growled Stan. 'This is our last night in Tokyo and all we want to do is get pissed.'

Pissed was an understatement. We were worse than the American had been by the time we'd finished the bottle of Bourbon and sunk a few beers somewhere else. We later had a vague recollection of two girls in a bar, getting into a taxi and going back to Camp Ebisu. In the morning, the orderly corporal had a devil of a job getting us up to catch the truck to the airport.

This time I didn't mind quite so much going back to Korea, for three reasons: I had a terrible hangover; Stan was with me; and there was the optimistic thought that a letter from Sylvia must surely be waiting.

15

But there was no letter from Sylvia waiting for me, only one from Mum. I said nothing, and neither did Stan. When it was our turn to go to the F-O-P, I found I was looking forward to seeing Manny.

He was very sympathetic but very much full of Sadie. 'I've done what you suggested,' he told me. 'I've sent a letter to my father.'

I started to get terrible pains in my stomach. They got so bad that Leggy told Stan to drive me down to the nearest US surgical hospital, and I was kept in overnight for observation for suspected appendicitis or ulcers.

The hospital was simply a large tent – as in the TV series *MASH* – with sixteen beds inside. Emergency cases were treated there until being flown to Tokyo. I was put in the bottom bed on the right-hand side. The other beds were occupied by wounded, brought in during the day and the previous night.

They lay there, a sorry-looking lot, in the glimmer of two paraffin lamps hung up on the central poles. I had been given two bottles of revolting medicine – one yellow, one red – to take before and after eating.

When the night rounds were completed it was decided that each soldier in turn should tell how he came to be there, starting with the bottom bed on the left-hand side, opposite me. This meant that I would be last.

'I was creeping along the Commo trench,' said the first GI, 'when a Chinky bastard jumped me and slid a knife into my back. I got my hands around his throat and I didn't care about the pain. I hated that little bastard so much that I was determined he was going to die. I squeezed with all my might. He struck me again, but my hands didn't belong to me anymore. They just kept on digging into his neck. Then I passed out. They told me afterwards that at first they thought we were both dead. I was still lying on top of his body with my hands round his throat.'

Many murmurs of understanding ensued after that little story. In the bed next to the GI with knife wounds, another GI lay unconscious. His mate, in the third bed, with a bulging bandage round his head, told their story:

'He was asleep when a mortar blew both his feet off. A piece of shrapnel took half my ear away.' His voice faltered slightly.

'God, it was awful! He jumped up and screamed and tried to run – but he didn't have any feet! I'll never forget it as long as I live. I can't imagine the agony he must have been in. He took a few steps, like someone on stilts, and screamed louder than ever. He fell over and lay there screaming until he blacked out.

'He got married just before we came out here. Now he'll be crippled for life.' His voice took on a vicious note: 'And all because of these yellow, stinking little bastards and their rat-infested country that wants blowing to hell.' His voice had almost reached hysterical level. Then he was silent.

The silence continued for a while until the next American broke it: 'I guess I'm unique. Do you know where I got shot? Straight between the balls!'

The funny side was much appreciated.

'No kidding,' he went on. 'I was running when the bullet hit me. It was just as if a gust of wind had sat me down with my legs out straight in front of me. Then the pain started and I looked down and saw the blood. I almost fainted clean away, I can tell you. Ruined for life, I thought. But, do you know, that little old bullet went right on through without touching anything vital. 'Course, it took some of my ball bag with it, but the doc tells me they'll graft me on a new one in Tokyo, and I'll be as right as day. But, Lordy, they're beginning to throb a bit now!'

My stomach pains eased as I listened to the rest of the stories. They had all been wounded, some heroically, in the course of action. Finally, it was my turn! I felt rather sheepish.

'As a matter of fact,' I said, 'I've got stomach ache.'

There was a heavy silence. Then the GI with the knife wounds called out, good humouredly: 'Hey, doc! We've got an English malingerer in here! Throw him out!'

Those who could, laughed. 'I reckon he ought to recite, sing or show his ring!' a GI shouted from the other end.

'Yeah!' cried someone else. 'Make the bastard!'

'All right,' I said. 'But I'd rather tell you a story about an English soldier called Pilkington. How about that?'

'OK,' was the response. 'But it had better be good.'

At the end of my story it took a second or two for the ending to sink in. Then laughter broke out. I was accepted, even if I did only have a tummy ache!

Next morning the GI without feet was found to be dead. As the body was carried out, his mate began to cry. I think all of us would have liked to have blown up all of Korea.

I was given another examination by the doctor.

'Well, you've got no ulcers and it's definitely not appendicitis,' he told me. 'Your stomach's in nervous disorder. You are living on your nerves too much. Try to let out some of your fear. Don't be ashamed of it. Also, and I know this may sound daft where you are, try to eat regularly, and keep taking the medicine. Don't go more than two hours, three at the outside, without eating. Now I'd better see about getting some transport fixed up for you.'

But he didn't have to bother. Stan arrived in the jeep to see how I was.

'So, what's wrong with you?' he asked, as I put my small pack in the back.

'Nerves and wind,' I told him.

He laughed. 'I've been farting like a dray horse. I don't think those Yankee tins of cold beans and frankfurters agree with me. I think they should be called frank-farters! Want to drive?'

'No, you can,' I said, and he started the engine.

As we set off, he said: 'I saw two Yanks get it last night. They were sitting on the skyline and lit up cigarettes of all things! Christ knows what hit them. Probably the same type of machine-gun that almost got us that time. It knocked them flying for yards. And do you know what Leggy said when I told him?'

I shook my head. 'What?'

'"Serve them fucking well right. I've told them enough times about it!"'

'Many shells last night?' I asked.

'Nope. Except for the machine-gun it was rather quiet. Perhaps Chinky's run out of ammunition. He's certainly been using enough.'

That night, the North Koreans showed they hadn't run out of ammunition by putting in an attack a little way over on our right flank. But no shells fell on Three Five Five. There was no moon but it was light enough by the stars to see where to walk.

'I don't think the Chinks will trouble us tonight,' said Leggy, 'so we'll take advantage of the stars and fetch those posts up from the bottom of the hill. Then they'll be ready for reinforcing the F-O-P. Sutton can keep watch at the F-O-P and McCleod will be in the observation post. We can bring the posts up the quick way, so long as we don't outline ourselves above the top of the ridge. It's pretty dark at ground level.'

'It's always the same,' I told him. 'When I did my night jump at Upper Heyford, I couldn't see the ground – or where the ground was – until I hit it. Yet those on the ground could see me quite clearly.'

Leggy and I worked on through the night. Manny came round in time to volunteer to take Leggy's place and carry up the last post – Leggy was puffing considerably.

'When you've brought that one up, you can call it a night and get your head down,' he told me.

Manny and I walked down the hill, frogs croaking on one side of us and shells and mortars flickering and crunching on the other.

'I used to love nights like this back home,' I said. I looked up at the sky with its millions of stars. 'I wonder what really is out there. What's the reason for it all and whether there really is a God, or something. Do you think there is?'

Manny looked up at the stars as well. 'Hell, I don't know what to think. It seems pretty vast for one person or thing to have thought up. And I prefer to believe science. It's something I can grasp.'

'Yes, but the problem is that nobody knows why it all happened. And that's where religion comes in and tries to give the answer. It sort of pounces on that as a last straw. Until science comes up with that answer, the old Church will still be going strong. But I'm never any good in a debate because I can always see and sympathise with both sides of the argument. For instance, in contradiction of what I've just said, that nobody knows why it all happened, Man has become so big-headed that he must have a reason for everything. Why can't it all have been a natural accident, starting from something that was nothing and evolving till the present day? Why does everything have to be neatly tied up with a concrete reason?'

I stopped and shook my head, smiling. 'Do you know what I think is wrong with me where the Church is concerned? I've just this minute realised it.'

'What's that?' asked Manny.

'Apathy. I don't like joining anything. I always want to be an individual. Perhaps it's because I was always set apart from other children because of my red locks and, because of it, usually made the centre of attention. Even now I am singled out. Look at those women in Tokyo. They went a bundle on my red hair. And because I want to be an individual I want to get out of the Army now.

'Every bloody little society has its own rules and regulations, the code of the old school tie, for example; and what with those and social laws, they're a bit too much for me. 'Course, lots of people lap them up. They're gregarious, like sheep, and they get a feeling of security out of them.'

'I think a lot like you,' said Manny, as we resumed walking. 'A lot of us do, back in the States. Youth wants to be free and have a voice. But, as somebody once said, no man is an island and people will always want to belong to some group or sect or other. It stems from the tribal system, and the group they belong to is their individuality.'

'I know,' I agreed. 'But take the night when Chinky fired rockets at us at The Hook, I was expecting to die every minute. They say a coward dies a thousand deaths and I certainly did, and have done all the while I've been out here. Although I say to myself that when I die it will be just like being knocked out for ever, there is always a flicker of hope at the back of my mind that there will be another life. Sometimes I wish I really could believe, belong to the Church and gain comfort as millions do; it would be so much easier then. I was once sent on a Christian Leadership course in the Harz Mountains in Germany, and I listened to the teachings of five theologians; but even with their superior brains and indoctrinations, I just couldn't accept it somehow.'

'It's pretty much the same with me,' said Manny. 'I think the best thing is to reconcile yourself to the fact that there's nothing else when you go. Then, if there is, just think of the lovely surprise you'll get. You don't know, they might really have it made over there. Look at all those gorgeous chicks who have died! They're probably holding fantastic orgies.'

'Or, of course,' I added, 'it could be Hell where all the beer barrels have got holes in them and the women haven't!'

'Hey! That's pretty good,' said Manny, laughing. 'I must remember that.'

I chuckled too. 'If there is a God, I'll look Him straight in the eye when I get there and tell Him, sorry, but you just didn't ring true to me at the time.'

'Yeah, I really believe you would,' said Manny.

'Did I tell you that my grandfather was a preacher? He was a Wesleyan – one of John Wesley's boys. He had only one arm. The other was sliced off in a chaff-cutter when he was sixteen. It was said that he had the finest set of teeth in the village. He used them for pretty near everything. Tying his bootlaces and harnessing the carthorse. And he would walk ten miles to the village of Winslow, deliver a sermon, then walk back. I'd like to see a parson do that today. When the village whore lay dying, she asked for the last rites. The village vicar, the old sod, wouldn't go. But my grandfather did. He said the poor, misguided woman was as worthy of last rites as anyone else, perhaps even more so.

'He reckoned it was no wonder that the Church of England was faltering if it allowed its religion only to a selected few. You don't know about the village church in England, but it can be pretty snobbish. Most women attend to show off their new hats. The attitude is the poor can look after themselves, we are nice and clean and holy.

'I think my grandfather was a bit of a revolutionary. He said the Church was too caught up in religion for religion's sake and it forgot the bit about goodwill to fellow men. And he always wanted to know why religion had to be so bloody mournful. He was probably a Salvationist at heart. I like their good old rousing songs. Hey! Do you know "Throw Out the Life-line, Someone is Sinking Tonight"?'

'Of course. I like that one,' said Manny.

He and I marched on down the hill, singing it for all we were worth and beating imaginary drums.

The last post happened to be the longest and heaviest. We sweated and puffed with it on our shoulders and stopped for a breather about halfway up. That was when the battery's mail orderly caught up with us.

'Got a letter for you, Kingy,' he said. 'I think it's the one you've been waiting for. It's postmarked Weymouth.'

Excitement tingled me. Sylvia often posted her letters from Weymouth.

'Boy oh boy!' I said, and grabbed it. I sniffed the envelope. 'No scent!' I moaned. But I laughed with joy and did a little dance.

'You're excused all I've been thinking,' I called out to the stars, and I waved the letter high and kissed it.

'That should keep him happy for a while,' the mail orderly commented to Manny, and walked on up the hill.

I tore open the envelope and took out one, small sheet of paper with only half a page filled with writing. A strange presentiment was already clutching me. I held the page so that the starlight fell on it.

What was written there was worse than any foreboding.

'Oh, no,' I whispered. Then I shouted it: 'Oh, no!'

'What in God's name's the matter?' exclaimed Manny. 'She's not dead, is she?'

I shook my head, blankly. Without a word, I handed him the letter. Sylvia was terribly sorry but she had met someone else. Was going to have a baby by him. Was three months pregnant and they were getting married. She could see now that it never was love that she'd felt for me. She knew I would understand and wished me a happy birthday for March 8th.

I turned away. I felt like crying, but I couldn't. Emptiness and loneliness filled me – and bitterness. Mum was right about no one needing to prove himself and her being sick of glory and honour. Trying to achieve those things had cost me the loss of Sylvia. And she certainly wasn't caring now whether I lived or died.

I allowed the bitterness to come through more forcibly, and it protected me against the hurt. I brought to mind and magnified all the little things about Sylvia that I disliked. And a strong, hard resoluteness and determination to go on gripped me. It was a resoluteness and determination that was also to serve me in good stead when three further such tragic endings to love affairs were to occur in my life.

'What a rotten little bitch!' Manny's voice cut through my thoughts. 'Fancy sending a "Dear John" letter like that.'

He touched my arm. 'Kingy . . .' he began.

I turned and managed a smile. 'I'm all right,' I said. 'I'm all right. Don't worry about it.' I turned away again. When next I spoke, my voice was very quiet: 'I know that in films, guys who get letters like this go berserk and go charging the enemy spraying sub-machine-guns. But it's OK. I shan't do anything like that.'

Once more I turned to face him. And back came the forced smile. I took the letter from him. 'Thanks,' I said.

Manny looked down at the post. 'I can go and get Stan to help me if you like,' he said.

'No. Let's get the bloody thing up there.'

When we had heaved the post with the others, Manny asked: 'You sure you're feeling OK?'

I nodded. 'Yes, I'm OK. Think I'll turn in.'

'Want any beer?'

168

'Nope.'

'Want a chaw?' I appreciated his attempt at humour. 'See you in the morning,' I said, and turned to go.

'Kingy . . .' I stopped and looked over my shoulder.

'Nothing much,' said Manny. 'Just – sorry.'

A myriad thoughts flew through my head until I fell asleep. In the morning, the memory of the letter hit me and again I felt like crying. I realised that my stomach ache had gone! It was either the shock, I thought, or the revolting medicine. When I showed the letter to Stan, he uttered the same sort of comments as Manny had done.

Manny joined me in the F-O-P during the afternoon watch.

'Why don't you go sick?' he asked me, seeing my face. 'If you told Leggy, he'd probably order you to have a rest behind the lines.'

'No. I don't want any rest. I'll be OK. But I've got to show that bitch that she hasn't hurt me. That's what I've got to do. Have you an envelope I could have?'

Manny went to his dug-out and fetched me one. I wrote Sylvia's name and address on it and printed 'Whore – *Third* Class' in the top left-hand corner. I wasn't going to give her the privilege of being first-class. Then I scooped up some Korean dirt, put it inside the envelope and sealed it.

'There,' I said, 'that'll show what I think of her!'

I laughed and so did Manny. A few hours later, Leggy came round to the F-O-P and motioned me outside.

'I'm very sorry about the letter,' he said. 'Sutton told me about it. It was not an uncommon thing in the last war. Look. I'm not going to order you, but I think you should go back down to the troop.'

Looking back on that moment, I think that the young have more resistance to broken love affairs. I certainly felt better with the envelope containing Korean dirt that I was going to post.

'I would rather stay here,' I said. 'We've been a team for quite a while, and Sutton and the American are people I can talk to. And I can assure you I'll be all right.'

'OK,' he said, 'but if it becomes too much, go. Rather, if I see you not doing your work properly, I'll order you to go.'

He smiled. 'But when Dog Troop relieve us I am sending you to Inchon. Then you'll be fresh for our next turn at the F-O-P.'

It was at Inchon that I got the chance to meet one of those Korean girls the American padre had warned us about.

And I took it!

16

In the earlier part of the Korean War, ships of the Royal Navy had bombarded Inchon as a softening-up process for an invasion. Now it was a rest home for Commonwealth troops. Rather like an English nursing home, it was run by matronly WVS. Fortunately the perimeter fence had a convenient escape hole for libertines.

On my first clandestine night out with three other lascivious soldiers, I took in many beers and a live sex show involving two grease-smeared Korean women who, with their enormous rolls of fat, resembled the Michelin tyre man.

'Christ!' I said to Freddy, a gunner from Dog Troop. 'That was enough to put anyone off sex for a week!'

He heartily agreed and, after sinking a few more beers in a bar, we crawled back through the hole in the perimeter fence to the sanctity of the camp.

Freddy, as I did then, believed in the body beautiful, and we spent many hours on the parallel bars and swimming in the lagoon that was cut off from the sea by a lock gate.

Although the nights were cold the days were very hot and the lagoon was tepid with the heat it retained from the sun.

Immersion went unnoticed because the water was the same temperature as the air. In fact it was like swimming in warm treacle.

One morning, Freddy and I were sitting on the beach on the other side of the lock gate, looking at the cool, inviting sea, and at a small, rock island about a quarter of a mile offshore.

'How about a swim out to that island?' he asked. 'It's not far.'

The sea, after the lagoon, was deliciously fresh, and we

swam, steadily, with me several yards in the lead. Suddenly, a huge fish leapt into the air in front of me. Being a true coward, I trod water until Freddy drew alongside.

'That was fucking big, Freddy,' I said. 'Fucking big.'

We swam on, shoulder to shoulder, and reached the island's shore. We discovered that the island was nothing more than sand, boulders and trees. Everywhere was shrapnel.

We found what resembled a trail and began walking along it to see what was on the other side. I was in front and looking, exploratively, to my right and left.

Suddenly, Freddy shouted: 'Stop! Don't move!'

There, just in front of me, was a giant spider's web, about a yard in diameter and completely blocking the path. In the centre of the web was a spider, as big as a tarantula but with hairless legs. Its belly was grotesquely bulbous and black. Uncontrollable shivers seized me at the thought of walking into that web.

Freddy and I stepped back and began throwing small rocks at the spider. It fled, leaving behind a tattered and passable web.

The other side of the island offered no other vista than the sea, and we lay down on the hot sand.

'Seeing that huge fish and the spider,' I said, 'reminds me of the time when dysentery hit us last year.'

'I remember that,' said Freddy, 'but I don't get the connection.'

Medically termed 'Twenty-four-hour dysentery', we had referred to it as 'Montezuma's revenge' and 'One step, two step, hop'. It struck like lightning and without warning.

'It got me,' I said, 'one sunny afternoon when I was sitting under the crest of a hill. An ant, black and about an inch and a half long, sauntered by. I never knew ants that size existed. I decided to watch and follow to see how far it was going to walk, and it went well over fifty yards! It found an enormous, dead black beetle. Holding the beetle above its head, the ant started back up the hill.

'It was then that I saw the toad and immediately thought of Conan Doyle's *Lost World*! That toad was about a foot high!'

'I know,' Freddy broke in. 'I've seen one. Terrifying.'

'I picked up a stick and poked it just to make sure it was real. And the damn thing grabbed the stick in its mouth and pulled real hard! Discretion being the better part of valour, I let go of the stick and left, hurriedly. It was then that Montezuma struck. I only just got my pants down in time. Did you get it in Dog Troop?'

'Yes,' said Freddy. 'Everybody did. It was strange how that evil-smelling green blob that came out twenty-four hours later signified the end of it. And it really putrefied the air!'

'I think all the little nasties lived in that green blob,' I said, 'and that was the end of them. But things here in this country are big. Have you seen the size of the snakes?'

He nodded. 'Huge aren't they? But I don't think they're poisonous.'

'No,' I said. 'I've been told they're pythons. They just crush you to death.'

We agreed that the Korean rat was normal, though, and conjectured that there must be many creatures in Korea that we never saw because of the noise of gunfire.

We dozed, and when we awoke the sea had gone right out. There was nothing but sand and mud between us and the mainland. We walked casually back and found that we'd almost missed lunch. An agitated WVS woman hurried over to us as we entered the mess hall.

'Where have you two been?' she demanded. 'We have been searching everywhere!'

We told her that we had swum over to the island, slept and walked back. She was horrified.

'Oh, you foolish boys!' she cried. 'Don't you know there are many sharks in these waters?'

We were both very subdued at that, and I told her about the big fish we had seen. 'You were very lucky,' she said. 'That wasn't a shark. It was probably a porpoise. Now, go and get your lunch, and don't you ever go swimming in the sea again. That is what the lagoon is for, and the lock keeps out the sharks.'

While we were eating, I said: 'Do you believe that bit

173

about sharks? It strikes me as peculiar that we weren't told, and why aren't there any notices?'

'That's a point,' he replied. 'Perhaps she just wanted to worry us for worrying her.'

On our sixth and last night, after we had been paid, Freddy and I exited once more through the hole in the perimeter fence. We were each equipped with a half-pound bar of milk chocolate, the recognised fee for the services of a Korean girl, so the Australians had informed us. After a few blatant enquiries we entered a house of sin.

It was nothing more than a hut in which lived a *mommasan* and her four teenage daughters. These were sitting on the floor, their naked feet stretched out to an iron pot in which glowed red-hot embers.

Smiling contentedly, the *mommasan* took the two bars of proffered chocolate and indicated that we should each choose a daughter. I picked a long-legged girl who had eyes more round than normal. She reminded me quite a lot of Sylvia.

Freddy chose a girl for himself and all four women knelt on the floor, smiling and chattering, and undid our laces and took our boots and socks off. We stood there, wondering where we were to go. Then I was led to one dark corner, and Freddy to another and blankets were spread on the floor.

In those dark corners, while the other two daughters and their mother sat round the fire-pot, munching chocolate, the dastardly deeds were done.

Two armed regimental policemen were waiting at the hole in the perimeter fence. 'Here come two more for the high jump,' said one of them. 'We're having a fine catch tonight.'

They took our names, rank and numbers and told us to report to the gymnasium at nine o'clock the following morning.

'There's not much they can do to us,' I said to Freddy, as we made our way to the barracks. 'The truck's leaving at two o'clock.'

There were more than thirty of us assembled in the gymnasium, the vast majority being Australian. 'Christ!' I exclaimed. 'There's nearly all the camp here!'

174

We were called to attention and a tall distinguished lieutenant-colonel entered. He told us to be seated.

'I am not going to punish you,' he said. 'Most of you will probably be punished enough later on. A new form of non-specific urethritis is running rife in Korea and so is syphilis. The former is showing resistance to penicillin and doctors fear for possible after-effects. But of course, syphilis is the terror. That can lay dormant in your system for many years.

'Those of you who are married will probably infect your wives; those of you who are not will probably meet a pretty girl one day and marry her, and she will become infected, too. Sometimes, syphilis waits and shows itself in the baby of an infected person. The baby can be born blind or with parts not quite right.

'Some of you have exposed yourselves to dangers that can ruin your future lives and happiness, and for what? A few moments of pleasure. I know you are from fighting units and that is why I feel damn sorry for you. If the opportunity arises again to mix with Korean girls, shun it. Use your hand for release, or, better still, use a friend's hand!'

'Dirty old queer!' murmured Freddy.

'Did someone say something?' The lieutenant-colonel stared hard at all of us. 'Very well, that's all I have to say. Dismissed!'

I didn't care much about any disease. I didn't have a girl back home any more, and the prospects of finding another one that I would want to marry seemed very remote.

I went to the WVS office, gave them my mother's name and address and the receipt for the fan I had bought. I was assured that they would contact Camp Ebisu and the fan would be sent to my mother, safe and sound.

17

'Well, how are we feeling? Fighting fit?' Leggy asked me when I got back to the troop.

'Much better, thank you,' I said. 'The good, regular meals were much appreciated. My stomach's as right as rain. When are we off to the F-O-P?'

'Ah, we're not – not to Three Five Five, that is.'

'Why? Where are we going? And I won't be able to say cheerio to Manny.'

'Back to The Hook,' said Leggy. 'And you wouldn't be able to say cheerio to that American chappie, in any case. He was shot dead by a sniper two days ago, right outside the F-O-P.'

I went to my dug-out and lay down on my bedding roll which Stan had prepared ready for me.

'Bloody bastard Chinks!' I snarled, and closed my eyes.

'That's a nice greeting, I must say,' said Stan. 'Oh, I take it you've heard about Manny. Tough, eh? What was Inchon like? Is it worth going?'

'Just shut up a minute, then I'll tell you. And thanks for doing my bedding roll.'

I kept seeing Manny and hearing him saying: 'Want a chaw?' Remembering our conversation about a possible after-life, I smiled with the hope that they *had* 'got it made over there' and that Manny was with one of those gorgeous chicks.

The hatefulness and irony of war, my thoughts went on. He'd had his Sadie, loving and waiting for him, and he was dead. I had no girl waiting for me, and I was alive.

But that smug feeling I knew so well was with me – that he was dead and I was alive. But don't get too smug, I told myself. There's still time and opportunity for you to be as dead as he is.

I turned over on to my right side and propped my head on my elbow. 'The first shall be last and the last shall be first, saith the Lord,' I said to Stan, 'and the last thing I shall tell you first is about a dirty old lieutenant-colonel . . .'

Except for the Royal Artillery, Commonwealth troops were still out of the line. The Americans were on The Hook, and it had deteriorated immensely during their weeks of intermittent occupation, for they had continually lost it to the North Koreans. It looked fit only for the rats that ran everywhere. The whole place stank of rotting dead.

'My Christ!' said Stan, as I aimed a kick at a rat that was trying to hide in a very dead armpit.

'Hmm!' said Leggy. 'I think we had better start digging, don't you? One consolation, the Black Watch will be back here shortly.'

'The sooner the better,' was Jock's comment.

'Why did we have to come down here, anyway?' I asked, as Stan and Jock pulled the dead GI a few yards away from the F-O-P.

'Because Intelligence has heard that the Chinks will be making a big move to retake The Hook once and for all,' Leggy told us.

'Why do we always have to go where there is going to be a battle?' grumbled Stan.

'We're the nomads of the line,' said Leggy. 'Our task is to support any unit that needs it. After all, there's not much point in directing shellfire where the enemy isn't! Don't you agree?'

'I suppose so,' replied a disgruntled Stan.

That night, I stood the midnight-to-eight watch. Unbeknown to us the Americans had installed a bank of rockets behind the crest of the hill at the rear of the F-O-P. About two thirty in the morning I thought my end had really arrived. The whole bank was suddenly fired, shattering the stillness with their whoops! whooshes! whoops! and illuminating everything fiery red all around, as though I'd been sent to Hades.

They roared right over my head, their red tails streaking across the valley. It took a second or two for me to realise that they were leaving and not coming in, and during that second or two they were almost as frightening.

I went out and grabbed an American by the arm. 'Why weren't we told about those bloody rockets?' I demanded.

He looked at me, blankly. 'You'd best see the lootenant about that,' he said, and resumed chewing.

'Do you know what they were firing at?' I persisted. 'It's our job to know.'

He shrugged, nonchalently. 'Probably a munition train, or a long-range gun. I heard the lootenant say we'd got some new sound-ranging gear, and they've probably been trying it out. I heard them say that it can pick up a gnat's fart at a hundred yards.'

'A gnat's fart — ' I began. But the thought of a tiny gnat passing wind was too much for me at that time in the morning. I was still laughing when I was back inside the F-O-P. When Leggy arrived just before six, I told him about it, and he chuckled.

'Typical,' he said. 'Typical.'

Dog Troop's men arrived to relieve us, and their reaction to the mess The Hook was in was the same as ours had been. And still the North Koreans held off their attack. We all reckoned that they were waiting for the Black Watch. And they were.

We were at the F-O-P when the Jocks arrived and started clearing up the 'filthy mess' and digging in deeper than ever.

Once more, loudspeakers warned the Black Watch of a terrible end; and 'that Sassenach Chinky woman', as Jock called her, serenaded us with 'Loch Lomond'.

Intelligence soon reported that an attack could be expected at any time. It came after a full day's very heavy shelling.

Jock McEwell's replacement, Gunner Pete Brindsley, was in the F-O-P. The rest of us were in the observation post having a welcome cup of tea. In readiness for the attack, Stan and I wore two bandoliers, criss-crossed over our chests. Suddenly, the bugles started going full blast.

178

'Drink up!' said Leggy. 'They're here!'

And he and I rushed to the F-O-P just as the first bullets came zinging in.

Like something out of *Viva Zapata*, I sped along the trench and dashingly entered the F-O-P. Unfortunately, I had forgotten something frightfully important – my rifle! I had one hundred rounds of ammunition, but no rifle!

'What *am* I going to do with you?' Leggy cried, in desperation. 'For Christ's sake go back and get it. You'll be the laughing stock of the British Army! And don't get killed on the way! You're needed here! Brindsley, you go with him and stay and give Sutton a hand.'

But with the ace that Leggy and the Black Watch had up their sleeves, I needn't have bothered about my rifle. I never even fired it.

Searchlights and flares suddenly blazed, lighting up the entire valley and the advancing North Koreans, who stopped, dazzled. Then machine-guns, stens and rifles began to rip them to pieces. I was on the phone all the time, directing the guns and mortars to Leggy's swift commands. It was the Jocks' battle and, with the enemy under the spotlight, they quickly finished it.

During the nights that followed, the Black Watch made many probes into enemy territory to try to get a prisoner for interrogation.

One night there was great excitement. The Jocks had got a prisoner! But he was shot trying to escape before Intelligence could question him. Other prisoners were taken and these quickly committed suicide. But the Black Watch did manage to keep one for interrogation. And it was learned that yet another attack was to come on The Hook.

A month went by and the Black Watch were withdrawn from the line. They were relieved by the King's Regiment and then by the Duke of Wellington's Regiment.

'Regiments come and regiments go,' said Stan, 'but we go on for ever. I reckon the mortars have had the arse-end of this war.'

'And we've still got it,' I told him.

We watched the Dukes come in. 'More lambs to the

slaughter,' I said. Not only were the majority of the Dukes under twenty years of age, they were mainly conscripts.

The King's, too, had been young, and green. On their first night they had sent out two inexperienced patrols into no-man's-land. One patrol heard a movement and blazed away at it. It was the other patrol – which quickly returned the fire. The tragic result was that the two patrols cut each other to pieces.

'The Dukes won't be so bad,' Stan informed me. 'Leggy says they've been in action before on a quieter part of the front.'

The Dukes weren't so bad either. Intelligence reported that the attack the prisoner had told them of, was to be the biggest The Hook had ever known. The Dukes sat and waited for that massive attack to come, each night growing sweatier with tension and anticipation.

As luck would have it, Dog Troop was at the F-O-P when it came. Even so, it was hell at the mortars, tucked in, in close support.

Intense shelling began in the evening and went on until dawn. It was later recorded that four thousand five hundred shells fell on The Hook that night, and for three days afterwards, two thousand shells fell in every twenty-four hours.

As though he had heard the words of Alabama, an English historian later wrote: 'It was more than flesh and blood could stand.'

But I always reason that all the attacks were as bad, such as the time we faced the horde with the US Marines; and probably this attack was recorded because an English unit had been there. After all, a person can only die once, and to that person it doesn't matter if one or five thousand and one shells fall.

The Dukes held firm and The Hook remained theirs. It cost them more than one hundred killed and many more missing and wounded. Dog Troop lost two men killed, and Stan and I were as pleased as Punch that we hadn't been up there!

When we took over, all around was devastation, as it

always was after a major battle. Dug-outs were flattened and communication trenches were caved in. The Korean soil had been blown into heaps everywhere, like sand in a desert storm.

The Dukes were relieved instantly. Begrimed, bewildered and proud, they handed over to the Royal Fusiliers.

Towards the end of May, Leggy said to me one afternoon, looking up at the sky: 'Won't be long now before the monsoon arrives.'

'God!' I said, with surprise, 'Is it really a year since the last one?'

The torrential rains had wrought havoc in the mountains and valleys, the cascading waters cutting ruts and taking earth from the roots of large trees, causing them to fall and be swept on to the River Imjin. The trunks had slammed and wedged themselves against the piles of a bridge the Royal Engineers had painstakingly erected, and, with the force of the risen water behind, the bridge gave and was swept away.

'Oh, the joy of mending telephone wires in the pissing wet!' Stan joined in.

Leggy nodded. 'It was three years ago, just as the monsoon started, that this nasty little war began. The North Koreans chose a good time to cross the 38th Parallel – most of the South Korean Army was on leave.'

'What is the history of this war?' I asked. 'No one has ever told me.'

'The United Nations instantly sent troops to help the South and the North Koreans were beaten back right up to the frontier with China. Then, in the November, two hundred thousand Chinese came to the aid of the North.'

'With the amount we've killed,' I pointed out, 'there can't be many of the bastards left now.'

Leggy looked at me. 'Do you know how many Chinese there are in this world?' he asked, sarcastically. 'Six-hundred million! Think about it!'

'What happened then?' I asked, ignoring the sarcasm.

'The South and UN troops were forced to retreat to the Seoul area. They regrouped and retook Seoul, and it was

181

decided to dig-in virtually astride the 38th Parallel. The Commonwealth Division was formed in the summer of 1951. You know the rest. After the Gloucestershire Regiment won its glory during the epic last stand on Hill Two Three Five, and the mortars died with them, this battery was formed as a bastard unit.'

'And I reckon we're a bloody fine bunch of bastards!' declared Stan.

'Five weeks later, we retook Castle Hill and Gloster Valley,' Leggy continued, 'and we drove on to the 38th Parallel and these present positions, some of which, as you know, are North of the Parallel. And that was the end of the mobile phase of the war.'

'And that's where I came in,' I said.

18

It was just over a week later, when we were at the mortars end, that two things happened which took me completely off guard and considerably upset me.

Stan was suddenly told to get his kit together. He was going home!

'There must be some mistake!' was all he could blurt out, in surprise.

But there was no mistake. His conscription was over. He was due for demob. I felt immensely pleased for him, yet sad and envious at the same time. I watched as his hands trembled with excitement, packing his clothes and personal effects.

'I told you I would get through,' he said, as we walked to the waiting truck. 'So will you. I'm sure of that. Who knows, probably one day we'll meet up in a pub somewhere and have a bloody good laugh about all this. Look after yourself, Kingy.'

'Yes. You, too. We'll keep in touch, eh?'

'Sure we will,' he said, as we shook hands. But we both knew we wouldn't. He got into the truck and he was gone. Sadly, I walked back to the dug-out and Stan's very vacant camp-cot.

A day or two later, Leggy went to see the medical captain. And he never came back! I was told that he had been flown to Tokyo as an emergency case for a long overdue operation.

To me it seemed as though the troop was going through a stage of metamorphosis. Charles was the next to go, quickly followed by Jock. They, too, were due for demob. Pretty Boy went shortly afterwards.

A Major Edwards took over as troop commander and F-O-P officer. A new F-O-P party was formed, with me being the only veteran. It wasn't at all the same and I felt uneasy and apprehensive at being surrounded by 'new boys'.

The Hook was still getting its daily quota of shells and, with the monsoon clouds that were forming, I grew more listless and tired each day. Major Edwards noticed this and after I had driven him recklessly through a hail of mortar bursts, his knuckles showing the whiteness of his face as he clutched the jeep, he asked me: 'How long have you been a forward observer?'

'Thirteen months,' I told him.

'Goodness gracious! Have you really? You've had enough of it, then?'

'Yes, I certainly have,' I replied.

'Very well. You are posted to Tactical Headquarters forthwith.' He smiled. 'You'll only *hear* the bangs down there. I should get your kit together straightaway.'

At Tactical HQ I found out what we pawns of the front line really meant to brass hats – nothing.

'If we sent a patrol out there, Nigel, we'd probably lose only ten men.'

'But, my dear Basil, better to send the patrol to this area. I know we stand the chance of losing nearly all of them, but look at the advantage and information we stand to gain.'

With their giant, green-velvet scale model of the battle area, they planned and played with their tin soldiers like little boys do. The only differences being that they smoked cigars, sipped whiskies and brandies and soda, and the little tin soldiers represented human beings.

How easy, I thought, scathingly, for them to order a front line unit to hold to the last men. They were surrounded by comforts, and they held the first means of retreat! It was all a game to them.

But their war games came to an end a few weeks later – on July 27th, 1953, when an Armistice was finally signed.

All brigades were drawn back behind a Demarcation Line, the Commonwealth troops together in one section. I went to see the 25-pounders to enquire after Jungle, and I was more than pleased to hear that he'd made it and was in Hong Kong. Then I visited the 1st Royal Tank Regiment because my mother had written that my two school chums, Eric and 'Nobby' Parrot, were in it. They were fraternal twins and looked as like as chalk and cheese.

I found only Eric. Nobby was on R-and-R in Tokyo. It was incredible and almost unreal meeting him out there. And I found out that his tank was one of those that came to our aid at The Hook!

'Fancy you being in that tin can only a few yards away!' I exclaimed. 'And I never knew!'

Whereas Nobby was always lugubrious, Eric was always full of humour. He loved to imitate an officer's voice. For a couple of years or so he had worked with me on the farm, and we recalled the day when a bull decided it didn't like us.

'Steady men,' Eric had said, in the tones of a leader of landed gentry class. 'Stay calm, men. I will deal with this. Have no fear. Stand resolute.' It was then that the bull charged. 'Run for your lives!' he screamed. And we both dived over the wall into the dung-heap! Then we both returned with pitchforks and gave the bull a damn good hiding.

Volunteers were asked for to help clean up no-man's-land. Bored and restless with nothing to do, I went along. As luck would have it, the party I was with went to The Hook. It was unbelievable, almost ghostly, venturing out on those brown, barren hills in broad daylight without any fear of being shot at.

But 'without any fear' is not strictly true. I just couldn't shake off the feeling of apprehension that possibly a few North Koreans hadn't heard that the war was over, and suddenly a gun would open up at us. I walked right over to the other side to see what our hills had looked like to the enemy. There was hardly any difference.

Everywhere in no-man's-land there was rotting flesh. A hand would be poking up, cold and ineffectual, from the brown soil. Sometimes it would be connected to a body; sometimes it wouldn't, the smashed part of the other end alive with white maggots and other crawly things.

Nearly all heads were without eyeballs. Carrion crows had had their fill. I noticed, too, that just as crows always pecked the arses of dead sheep and other animals, so they had done to dead soldiers. When we uncovered and lifted bodies with special close-tined forks, flies and long, brown beetles would stream out of all orifices.

A young conscript, who had joined the troop only a few days earlier, kept by my side, asking all sorts of awe-inspired questions. He caught sight of a giant of a Chinaman who lay with a bugle on his chest, and made a bee-line for him. The conscript snatched up the bugle as a souvenir. Then he was almost sick. The body and clothing were so rotten that half the chest came away, sticking to the bugle. The chest cavity was heaving with beetles and maggots. The stench of escaping gas was terrible.

I helped the conscript to clean the bugle. 'For more than a year I've listened to these fucking things being blown,' I told him. 'First time I've seen one close up.'

'Do you want it?' he asked.

'No. You keep it. You saw it first.'

The task of cleaning up no-man's-land of its too rotting flesh took longer than one day. But I didn't volunteer to go back again. Neither did the conscript.

Chicken had been served to us on our return. The conscript got a leg. He was about to put it to his mouth when the memory of maggots and beetles came flooding back. Silently, he handed the leg to me. In complete understanding, I took it.

A few days later I received the news I had been waiting thirteen long months for – I was being posted to Singapore to finish my time. Oh, why couldn't Sylvia have waited, I thought, sadly and foolishly, to see me now I had won my glory. Who could I show off to now? Mum certainly wouldn't be interested. I had no one to be proud of me. But, perhaps, Mum *would* be. After all, she had been proud of Murray and Geoffrey. And besides, I cheered myself, I was proud of myself, and that was most important of all.

The night before I was due to leave, my name appeared on standing orders as guard commander. I thought how ridiculous it was to have guards when there was no longer an enemy.

Among the officers who left that evening to visit other regiments was a young, toffee-nosed subaltern who had arrived only that day. I ticked off all personnel as they returned, but well after midnight the subaltern was still absent. About two in the morning, I said to the guard: 'That bastard won't be coming back now. Probably too pissed to drive. Come on, let's get our heads down.'

Toffee-nose came back at three thirty and found us all asleep! I was instantly put on a charge. Next morning I appeared before Major Edwards. 'I'm sorry,' he said, 'after your record and service out here, but I must punish you. And with the truck waiting to take you, I can do only one thing. Reduced to the ranks. March out.'

The Transit Camp at Pusan wasn't far from the Military Cemetery. Everyone was expected to go there and pay their respects to the fallen. The last night in Korea was allocated to this. But I didn't go.

Nearly two million men had died in Korea. I could quite easily have been one of them. But I wasn't. I was alive. I wanted to be with the living. Not linger and meditate, mournfully, with the dead. They'd gone. There was nothing anyone could do for them.

I had won through the degradation of war, living most of the time like a filthy animal and facing a constant enemy. Nothing in life could ever be taken seriously after that. There seemed to be no point in it. Nothing could ever be *frightfully* important. Life was just a game, completely without reason. I would just regard my future life as a bonus. A gratuity of borrowed time.

I went out and found myself a South Korean girl who took me to the outskirts of Pusan where she lived with her family in a mud, straw and wooden hut. She fed me saki till I was too drunk to stand. I had a vague idea of love-making on the floor where her brothers and sisters slept between torn blankets and her mother and father looked on.

I awoke with the sun in my eyes and a heavy weight on my chest. This is where I came in, I thought, but I'd heard no Yorkshire voice of victorious exclamation. Instead, a steady 'tock, tock-tock' came to my ears. I raised my head and met the piercing eyes of an old cockerel, roosting on my chest. Hens were scratching and pecking the earth floor around me. And I started to laugh, joyously.

'Degradation to the fucking end!' I said.

19

My final look at Korea also presented a picture of degradation. The summer sun was dipping and had turned to an orange ball in a shimmering sky when the small troopship I was on pulled away from the Pusan dock.

A bare-footed little girl, in a tattered and faded frock, stood on the hot, tarred boards of the jetty, waving a grubby hand. I had seen many like her in the streets but this one looked more forlorn, wistful and alone. I wondered what her story was. Why was she there? Was she looking for a father killed in action?

Suddenly, she was attacked by Montezuma's Revenge. Hoisting her frock above a bare bottom she squatted. Apparently unmindful of the yellow liquid spurting from her like custard and curling itself round her toes and feet, she continued to wave, the yellow pool growing alarmingly wider and wider as though she were melting.

Sad, bitter and disgusted I turned my back and headed for the ship's bar. For me it was the final straw. I never wanted to see Korea again, and I never have.

That poor, wretched little girl with acute diarrhoea or dysentery summed up and epitomised all that Korea represented to me: a cesspit of a country that openly showed the scars of a civil war. I really hated Korea at that moment, even though it had accorded me the self-satisfactory glory I had sought.

Now, at last, I was rid of Korea and the clinging closeness of its brown soil. Free! I had blood on my hands but I was free: like a man who had spent more than a year in a prison's Death Row and had suddenly been reprieved.

When I got between the clean linen sheets that night I was very drunk but sublimely happy.

Two or three days later I once more set foot on the Land

of the Rising Sun. But the sun, like most people in the naval port of Kure, had gone to bed when we arrived. Next day, in the transit camp, I was told more details about my posting to Singapore. I would be holding courses in electronics and signals for junior officers. HM Aircraft Carrier *Unicorn* was leaving in two days' time to make her last voyage to a British 'graveyard' for scrapping and she would drop me off.

That night I decided to see what Kure had to offer: hundreds and hundreds of prostitutes! The pavements immediately outside the dock gates were as crowded with them as Piccadilly was on a Saturday night. Arthur Helliwell would certainly have been inspired to write another article!

Proudly displaying the Korean and United Nations war ribbons above my left breast-pocket, I swaggered through them, warding off their clutches and ignoring their offers of a thousand to fifteen hundred yen for an all-night session. My pass was only until midnight; besides which, I didn't see anything I fancied.

I made my way to the even brighter lights of the town centre. Four bars and as many John Collins later I found what I had been looking for. She was as well-upholstered as the bar seat she was perched upon and displayed nicely rounded calves and knees. She was, to use the old joke, the sort of girl you could take home to mother – if you could trust your father!

She instantly swung round towards me as I eased myself into the next seat. Ostentatiously she uncrossed her long legs, lifting her black silk skirt as she did so and allowing me a glimpse of a pink-ribboned suspender clasp.

'Hello,' she warmly welcomed me. 'Buy me a drink?'

I did so and she led me over to an alcove and sat closer than close to me.

'You want good time with me?' she asked. 'Three thousand yen all night.'

I looked at my watch. Nearly ten o'clock. 'I'm sorry,' I said. 'I'd really love a night with you, but I have to be back in camp by midnight.'

Without warning she kissed me and put my hand under her skirt on to her stocking-tops.

'I give you quickie for two thousand yen,' she whispered seductively. 'We go upstairs. No pay for bed.'

The average London rate as I had known it for a 'short time' was fifteen shillings (seventy-five pence). She was asking for double that, and I told her so.

She laughed. 'That OK,' she said. 'If you man enough, fuck me two times! Then you get London – how you say? – rate!'

I laughed, too. She kissed me again, my hand went higher and she touched me on my trousers where the sapling yearned for a hot, moist environment.

'Come on!' she urged. 'We have enough time. I keep my stockings on for more excitement.'

Just under an hour later I staggered back down the stairs to the bar in need of resuscitation. I was proud with accomplishment but decidedly deflated. For the next forty minutes I sank a John Collins every ten minutes, then lurched outside and grabbed a taxi. I didn't need to tell the driver to step on it. And I was too drunk to care.

I'll never know if that taxi-driver did it deliberately. He parked with the wheels touching a monsoon ditch on the side I was to get out. I paid him, opened the door – and pitched into three inches of water and about a foot of black mud! He drove off with a squeal of tyres.

The gate sentry – a young conscript – hastily levelled his rifle at the thing that was approaching and trying, ineffectually, to clean two war ribbons with a mud-coated hand and sleeve.

'Halt!' he croaked. 'Who goes there? Friend or foe?'

I'd always thought it was a damn stupid question, so I did something I'd always wanted to do.

'Foe! You bloody moron!' I snarled. 'Go on, shoot me!'

A short silence, then, timorously and deprecatingly: 'Who is it, really?'

'Me!' I retorted, and walked on by him to check in at the guardroom.

Suppressing humour and wrinkling his nose, the orderly officer told me: 'You deserve to be charged with defacing the Queen's uniform. All sorts of nasty and revolting things

– including yourself – find their way into monsoon ditches. I think the part you fell into must have been culturing for quite a while.' He turned, conversationally, to the guard commander. 'What do you think, Sergeant? What odours do you detect in the stench that is before us? I think, first, a mixture of rotted vegetation and decomposition of meat – a dog or cat or both – and, ah, yes, a very well-used sanitary towel. The cocktail is further enhanced by a dash of human faeces and a plentitude of piss, and, to cap it all, a strong injection of human vomit.'

Laughter followed me as, ingloriously, I made my way to the shower house. I removed my watch, pay book and money and got under the warm spray fully clothed.

Shortly after getting into bed I began to laugh, uncontrollably.

'Boil your head!' an irate voice growled from the adjacent bed. 'What the hell's so funny at this time of night?'

'Just a memory,' I replied, still chuckling. 'Go to sleep.'

'That's what I'm bloody well trying to do!' was the rejoinder.

The memory was of the evening Pug let me have his beloved civilian suit for a very special date in Salisbury, Wiltshire. It was a very well-cut, grey pin-stripe.

'Promise me you'll look after it, Kingy,' he had said, meticulously brushing the back and shoulders. 'It cost me a lot of money. I don't want to see a stain or even a speck of dust on it when you get back. Good luck with Jeanette. I hope you get your end away.'

But I had no luck with Jeanette. She wanted a ring on her finger first. Calling her a 'prick-teaser' and feeling highly frustrated, I left, and just managed to catch the last bus to Andover. But there were still four or five miles to camp and no more buses.

I was looking for a car to borrow when a milk tanker crawled by me on the long hill leading out of town, so I promptly hopped on to the back. There was another hill where the camp was and I reasoned that this would slow the tanker sufficiently for me to hop off. But I was wrong. On the flat between the hills, the driver really put his foot down. The momentum hurtled the tanker past the camp gates at a good thirty miles an hour, and it was keeping to the centre of the road!

I leapt off but didn't make the grass verge. Parachutist's roll or no, tarmacadam is not meant to receive a body at thirty miles an hour. The forward left roll I executed was perfect – feet first and turned to the right, body twisted to sink on to outside calf, thigh and buttock, a further twist to receive continuing impact diagonally across my back and, finally, on my right shoulder.

Maintaining some form of dignity I limped past the sentry to the guardroom. A mutual friend was on duty.

'My God, Kingy,' he gasped. 'Pug will murder you when he sees his suit!'

'I know,' I said, with a grin, 'but any PJI [Parachute Jumping Instructor] would have been proud of that roll.'

When I got to our Nissen hut I called out through the closed door: 'Pug! I don't want you to be upset, but I've got a speck of dust or two on your suit. I'm coming in. Now, don't be upset. I can explain.'

I thought at least he would hit me. But, after a cry of horror he lay face down on the floor, beating it with his fists, knees and boots. Then he rolled on to his back and began laughing. Everyone joined in – and so did I.

It was understandable. I'd seen myself in the full-length mirror at the guardroom. Apart from milk, blood and tar stains, the left trouser-leg was ripped open from turn-up to hip and the back of the coat was a series of upside-down 'L' rips. But the *pièce de resistance* was the inside, white, padded epaulette. This had been wrenched out of the right shoulder and was hanging down to my elbow!

'Jesus!' said Pug. 'She must have put up one hell of a fight!'

And off we all went into peals of laughter once more.

The deep channel to the open sea from Kure lies through a maze of high, verdant islands. Beneath a blazing, mid-afternoon sun I stood on the *Unicorn*'s flight deck, drinking in the ozone and feeling blissfully happy. I was on my way back to England with a few months' holiday in Singapore en route.

By my side was a young radar operator called Johnny.

'This part of the world is very beautiful, don't you think?' he asked.

'It certainly is, especially to me after looking at brown, shell-torn soil month after month. I've never seen such greenery.'

As the ship made her way very slowly between two very high and very close islands, perspective made it appear that I could spread both arms and touch each one. All the islands seemed to be virginal and uninhabited, and I thought, surely, this was how the world had been before Man's dominance and greed changed it under the pseudonyms of civilisation and progress. Nowhere was evidenced the three terrible Ps: Power, Politics and Pollution.

The islands looked vibrant yet drowsy, still yet with movement, quiet yet with noise. I thought that here was somewhere where a man could live with a good woman and without newspapers and radio and, as the song says: Let the Rest of the World Go By.

I had no way of knowing then that, twenty-three years later as I sat in a drunken stupor under an olive tree in Italy, the memory of those islands and the impression they had made on me would influence me to make a decision that changed my life entirely. (*The Islander*, New English Library, 1984.)

I had been mixed in as crew on the *Unicorn* and, to pay for my passage, I was given the distinguished tasks of galley slave and cleaning the 'heads' (lavatories). A hammock, which I fell out of only once, was slung next to Johnny's, and I spent many an hour swinging in it and watching the antics of the hundreds of long, brown cockroaches that were accepted as part of a seaman's life on the spotlessly clean ship.

Leisure-time, of which there was plenty, was well catered for. Sunbathing on the flight deck was a favourite in the daytime, or going aft to watch the officers banging away with shotguns at claypigeons. I thought that most of the officers were lousy shots.

There were no aircraft on board and one hangar was used as a gymnasium, another as a cinema showing first-class up-to-date films, and the third was a garage for officers' cars! A very important feature was the bar counter.

One afternoon as we lay on the flight deck, our bodies soaked with sun-tan lotion and sweat, I commented to Johnny: 'I should have taken my elder brother's advice and joined the Navy.'

'Why?' he asked.

'Well, you buggers have really got it made. Wherever you go, you have your comforts with you. Always hot water to hand and you never have to wipe your arse on a piece of old paper or a dock leaf. And you get your hot meals served on time. Have you ever eaten tins of cold spaghetti in tomato sauce or fatty bits of pork in cold baked beans?'

He laughed. 'No, and I hope I never have to. But I have been told that it is a terrible thing to be on a ship in battle because you know you are the only target and you can't run anywhere to safety. The only other place for you is Davy Jones's Locker.'

'I know,' I said. 'My brother always said that, but I've been thinking about it quite a lot since I've been on board. For instance, only direct hits can do the damage. Misses are cancelled out by the sea. I was told at the ballistics school that if you are swimming two-foot-six under water and someone fires a .303 at you from above the surface, you are safe. Therefore, the sea must deaden and stop shrapnel from spreading laterally but not the pieces that are shot up in the shortest, vertical line of expanding gas. So a miss of thirty yards is as good as the proverbial mile. But a miss of thirty yards on land can make you very much dead, and earth and stones become missiles too. A shell bursting on a solid rock face can kill you at sixty or even eighty yards. Anyway, that's my theory about the sea, and if it is so, which seems logical enough to me, and taking as an accepted fact that there are always more misses than direct hits – or I wouldn't be alive today – you buggers must have an edge on us Army blokes. And, on top of which, you have your comforts with you.'

'If you say so, Kingy,' he murmured, drowsily. 'I don't know anything about ballistics and I've never been in a battle, and I'm going to sleep.'

Kingsland, I told myself, you are becoming a bore and big-headed. Watch it! Next thing, you'll be bragging and boasting like the Yanks!

I'm not sure exactly when, but I think it was the day after we had passed the long island of Formosa, now called Taiwan, that I experienced a real thrill at sea.

Johnny and I, like many others, were taking our daily constitutional round the flight deck after lunch and were astern when a black dhow was sighted off the port bow.

The ship's megaphones suddenly came to life. 'This is the captain speaking,' a voice said, quite pleasantly and informally, 'I'm stepping up to twenty-two knots and going to see what a small craft like that is up to so far off shore.'

Not only was the acceleration terrific and exhilarating but the wheel was swung over hard to port and the deck, stretching out in front of us like a giant surfboard, dipped left towards the sea at such a crazy angle I thought we would topple over.

Then the spray was flying over the bow and coming back to soak us, and we were charging down on that black speck like some grey monster from the pen of Jules Verne.

Johnny told me that Jimmy – as Royal Navy skippers were invariably called – was having his fun. When we were close enough to see, the black dhow's crew was waving frantically at us; and still we bore down on that small craft until I thought that surely we must cut it in half.

Then, at the eleventh hour, as it were, Jimmy once more ordered the wheel to be swung over hard and he expertly cut engines. And there we were, riding nicely alongside.

Satisfied it was only a fishing boat, in no difficulties and 'not up to mischief', Jimmy resumed course for Hong Kong to take on fresh water.

I went ashore and made straight for the Royal Artillery barracks. But, disappointingly, I was told that Jungle was on a tour of duty in the Northern Territories. I decided against visiting Angela, Jungle's wife, and wrote a short letter to Jungle that I had 'made it' and was going to Singapore. I didn't mention Sylvia. Then I took the famous funicular railway to the top of Kowloon and drank in the view.

I had insufficient money to drink in anything else – not even an 'all-in tea'! There was a week to go before I would reach Singapore and be paid, and I needed what little money I had for cigarettes and refreshments on board.

We were about midway between Hong Kong and Singapore when, one late afternoon, our attention was excitedly drawn to a waterspout far off the starboard bow. Like a brown, bent Tower of Babel it soared to the heavens, sucking up the sea water and any fish that happened to be in its racing path.

Once again the captain's voice came over the megaphones, telling us he was going to make a very wide detour in case that 'extremely nasty thing' should suddenly decide to alter course and head towards us.

Even so, that night we encountered a very heavy sea and strong winds. Next morning, the sea was worse and it was my turn to wash up the breakfast things in a hot, smelly and gyrating galley. The water in the large and lip-rimmed washing-up trough was speckled with grease blobs and pieces of fried bacon rind began shooting backwards and forwards more violently. Despite the lip-rim the water was thrown over the sides on to the floor, and several pieces of crockery were flung from their slots and my hands and ended up in smithereens. Yet, throughout, my stomach remained serene!

When we emerged from the storm and I told Johnny I hadn't been seasick, he complimented me on being a 'good sailor'.

20

Although publicity about it in Britain had virtually died, there was still a spiteful, wearisome war going on in Malaya. A war of ambushes in dense, steaming jungle and of bullets in the back. And all the time, British soldiers were dying, all for the sake, so I was told, of the wealthy rubber planters.

A song, to the tune of 'The Red Flag', was openly sung about the situation and ended:

> But there'll come a day when you'll see
> Those planters down on bended knee;
> But they can go and kiss my arse,
> I'm on the homeward boat at last.

But the island of Singapore, separated from the true war zone by a causeway, was, I decided, a soldier's paradise; though it was a few weeks before I acclimatised to the intense, humid heat. It was like living in a sauna that became even hotter at night.

I was based in Nee Soon Transit Camp and placed on the semi-permanent staff. The camp had its own private swimming pool and a NAAFI – standing, of course, in the jocular sense for No Ambition And Fuck-all Interest – where one could drink, among other things, ice-cold 'Tiger' beer. A very potent brew, it was also named 'Fighting Beer' and it was claimed that after three pints you would cheerfully knife your best mate!

Then there were the 'Worlds' in the town itself – a New World and an Old World, as I remember them – which were giant fair and pleasure grounds, or 'dens of iniquity', where sex with a capital S was catered for by live shows, films, pimps and a cosmopolitan assortment of prostitutes.

There were also hotels and brothels specialising in fifteen-year-old girls imported from Bangkok. In the town centre there were two main social centres – for the wealthy, Raffles Hotel, which still stands; for us, the Nuffield Centre, which has been pulled down. The Nuffield had a giant indoor swimming pool – to keep the heat out – and a dance-hall with beautiful Singhalese hostesses to keep the heat in! Unfortunately, one of the girls was murdered just before I arrived and they had stopped going home with soldiers.

My duties consisted solely of holding two classes a day, five days a week, from eleven to twelve in the morning and from four to five in the afternoon. The rest of the time was mine. But, at first, the classes were anything but easy-going and sometimes I wondered how the majority of young British officers I was trying to teach ever got through the War Office Selection Board.

A Sergeant Foster, known as Fosty and who was as dried-looking and bony as Gandhi, was acting-quartermaster and personnel officer. After my first week he enquired how the classes were going.

'Bloody hard work,' I said. 'If some of those officers' brains were gunpowder they wouldn't have enough to blow their hats off! Either that or they just don't want to know about molecules, atoms and electrons.'

'I'll have a word with the RSM,' said Fosty. 'He'll shake the bastards up.'

A regimental sergeant-major has full command over all subalterns. I don't know what ours said or did but the officers were much more attentive afterwards. Then that batch left, another batch arrived, and the RSM was called upon to 'have words' again.

It was a lovely, lazy life – no parades or bullshit. Just an eight o'clock roll call in the mornings which everyone had to attend. I quickly fell into a routine of whoring and drinking when I had the money, and swimming and sun-bathing when I hadn't. I was more than determined to make up for those months in Korea.

There was another form of relaxation which I very much enjoyed. Our char-wallah was an Indian called Abdul: a wise old man and a devout student of philosophy. I spent many a hot afternoon in the cool of his small 'basher' – grass and bamboo hut – smoking his hookah with him and just talking.

One Wednesday afternoon when I was absolutely broke I said to him: 'I could really do with the services of a good woman.'

'Why you always want fuck woman?' he asked, quietly. 'Woman not necessary. Many more important things in life. You need pure mind. If you forget woman you find freedom – emancipation. Secular problems gone. Monks happy people. Man ruled by cock unhappy – not good.'

'You may be right,' I replied, 'but don't forget what our Bible encourages us – go forth ye hence and multiply. And multiplication really appeals.'

He chuckled. 'You incorrigible. No hope for you. You condemned to torment.'

'You just let me choose my own torment. And nothing, I am sure, is going to change the feeling in my loins.'

'You lose balls, you change,' he retorted with another chuckle.

'That's a terrible, wicked thing to say, Abdul. Look, there's a beautiful German girl in a particular hotel down town. She has white-blonde hair and her every movement excites me.'

'Well, go fuck her,' he replied.

'That's not what you were advocating just now.'

He shrugged. 'Like I said, you incorrigible. No hope. I turn my back on you.'

'Listen,' I said. 'This creature that I'm absolutely wild about wants forty dollars. She's really high class.'

He whistled. 'More than month wages. I no have forty dollars.'

'I'm not asking you for it. But there's a housey-housey session in camp tonight and I feel very lucky. I really believe in Lady Luck. I've entered many a card school with her on my shoulder and walked away with the kitty. And I really feel that she'll be with me tonight.'

'Go housey-housey.'

'That's just it. I'm flat broke.'

200

He studied me through a puff of hookah smoke. Then his whole black face wrinkled with a broad smile. 'I lend you five dollars. But you pay me back, mind, or no more tea and free smoke for you!'

'Abdul,' I said, 'you're a bloody good friend. I won't let you down. I promise.'

And I didn't let him down. Lady Luck took the first 'full house' for me, and I walked away with one hundred and forty dollars! I handed Abdul ten.

'It is sin money,' he said. Then he grinned: 'But I take it.'

I had already spruced myself up in the sure assumption that I would win. Fosty had managed to find a new red beret my size and this complemented nicely my green linen safari uniform adorned with the two ribbons and paratrooper's wings. I had blancoed the two courtesy, unpaid stripes I had been given back to teach the officers. I felt and looked very good.

Tingling with excitement, I walked down to the main road and grabbed a taxi.

When I entered the plush hotel's palm lounge that was cooled by large ceiling fans, I was instantly crestfallen. She wasn't there.

'Have you seen the blonde German girl?' I asked the red-coated bartender.

He looked at the wall clock. 'No,' he replied. 'But it's a bit early for her.'

I ordered a John Collins and went over to one of the red-curtained windows and sat down on a Regency-style sofa. A blue-coated waiter brought my drink and a large tray of cashew nuts, strips of raw, spiced fish and potato crisps. Another John Collins later she arrived. She looked absolutely delicious, sensuous and stunning in a white and black polka-dot silk dress, drawn taut over the thrusting points of her breasts by a thin, black patent leather belt round her trim waist. The skirt of the dress was full and, as she walked, it swirled and caressed her legs which were encased in glossy, black, nine-denier stockings of glass nylon. Her well-coiffeured hair was swept up under a large, sloppy-brimmed picture hat, also of polka dots. From her tiny ears

201

hung gold and pearl earrings. Completing the blood-stirring ensemble were black and white stiletto-heeled sandals and a black leather handbag.

The lounge was still almost empty. She saw me and came over smiling. I stood up, returning the smile.

'So,' she said, 'you've come back. I thought you would. I take it we are in the money tonight?'

I tapped my breast pocket. 'In that case,' she went on, in a German accent that made her voice even more sexy, 'I will have a dry sherry.' And she sat down next to me. I signalled to the waiter.

Taking a sip of her sherry she regarded me with hazel eyes over the top of the glass. She lowered the glass. 'I'm absolutely starving!' she exclaimed. 'Do we have enough for a really nice meal?'

'A pleasure,' I told her, feeling as flush as Lord Rothschild.

The hazel eyes sparkled. 'I can assure you, my darling, it will be. There is nothing like good food and wine to put me in the mood for love-making. The restaurant here is fabulous, and we don't have far to go afterwards. I have a room upstairs.'

I allowed her to choose from the menu, after I'd seen that the prices were not as expensive as I had feared. First, she ordered a Moselle white wine that was served from an ice bucket. For starters we had Italian-style whole tomatoes stuffed with rice and spices. A main course of Lobster Thermidor followed, with another bottle of Moselle. Then came a cheese board, ice-cream, port for me, brandy for her, then coffee and her Black Russian cigarettes.

During the meal I learned that her name was Lili – Lili Marlene, I called her – and she was born in Baden Baden. When the war in Europe ended she was seventeen and an orphan. Prostitution was the only way she could think of to survive. In 1950, after she'd found her way to West Berlin, an American Army officer took her to Paris. She left him and went to Nice, then to Marseilles. There she met a Swedish sea captain who took her with him on his tramp steamer.

'When we arrived at Singapore four – no five – months ago I knew this was where I wanted to live. Max, the Swede, was very kind. He gave me all the money he could afford to put me on my feet . . .' She giggled. 'Or, rather, on my back! I bought the sexiest and best clothes, booked into this hotel and – here I am.'

'But what about the future, Lili?' I asked. 'You can't be a prostitute all your life.'

'Why not?' she countered. 'I intend to reach the highest level of my profession.'

'What's that?'

'My darling, don't you know? Wife of a millionaire, of course. I am looking for him. I have saved my money. If I do not find him here, I will go to the United States of America.'

Her room upstairs was a suite! Lavishly furnished and, like her, it was totally seductive and feminine.

'Darling,' she cooed, taking off her hat and unpinning her hair, 'I don't want to sound commercial but, please, the money?'

I gave it to her and she went to the bathroom, calling to me over her shoulder to open the champagne we had brought with us.

When she returned she had removed her dress and looked ravishingly desirable in what she had worn beneath – black silk camiknickers, stockings and suspender-belt. Kicking off her sandals she lay back on the settee, spreading her legs in a wide vee. Then she slowly undid the two crotch buttons of her camiknickers.

'Pour a little champagne into me here,' she whispered, pulling up the laced hem of the cami-knickers. 'It will be delicious.'

She jerked as the ice-cold champagne touched her. And then, wild with desire, I drank from the best champagne glass that was ever invented.

Lili had set the bedside alarm clock for five o'clock, giving me, as she said, time for morning love-making before I had to return to camp. After I had showered, dressed and drunk coffee with her, I gave her a big kiss on her forehead and put two five-dollar bills down the front of her very sexy nightie.

'Thank you for a beautiful night,' I told her. 'I would really like you to find your millionaire.'

Abdul spat and called me a 'filthy bugger' when I told him about the champagne.

'You no more suck my hookah!' he cried.

But I did – after I had given him another five dollars.

I never went back to see Lili. As Confucius said: Parcel has no more excitement when you know contents. And that particular parcel carried a stamp duty of forty bucks!

21

I always preferred to go down-town alone. That way I could go where I liked and not be handicapped by the persuasions of others. I suppose, really, I was looking for a replacement for Sylvia. But I never found her in Singapore and always ended up with the most attractive woman I could afford.

In the morning I would hop on a workers' bus to get me back for roll call and weather the accusing, smiling eyes of the Malayans, for they knew full well what I had been doing.

One morning, Fosty saw me walking up from the main road. 'A word of warning, Kingy,' he said. 'I wouldn't go out on my own so much if I were you. Terrorists mix freely with people in Singapore. You could be sitting beside one and you wouldn't know. And he'd have no hesitation about slipping a knife into you.'

But still I continued to be a lone wolf. Then a Yorkshireman, who reminded me of Stan, arrived at Nee Soon, waiting to be posted to Kuala Lumpur. He attached himself to me and, finally, I relented and allowed him to go down-town with me.

We were sitting in a bar and the Tiger beer was hitting both of us, him more so than me. A giant of a soldier in the Argylls barged in and sat with his beer a few tables from ours.

Suddenly, the Argyll began sobbing and thumping the table.

'Ooooh!' he wailed. 'All my mates killed in an ambush. Everyone shot down in cold blood. The bastards were waiting for us. We never stood a chance.' He thumped the table top a few more times, and tears streamed down his cheeks.

'Oh, what am I going to do? I was the only one who escaped. Why? Why was I allowed to live and they are all dead?'

He started to scream like a maniac, and I never saw a bar empty so quickly. There were just the three of us left. I was quite content to sit it out and finish my beer, and let him get over his tantrum.

But Yorkie, with the Tiger inside him, did an impromptu and silly thing.

'Shut up, you stupid cunt!' he yelled.

The thumping and screaming stopped, and the hulk slowly turned to look at us, his red eyes full of hatred. I met them levelly while Yorkie, instantly regretting what he had done, sank down in his chair, pretending he wasn't there. The hulk moved very quickly for his size and a huge hand clamped down on my shoulder. He completely ignored Yorkie.

'Right. You,' he told me. 'Outside!'

He marched out through an open door at the rear that led into an unlit beer garden. I drained my glass and stood up.

'Now look what you've done,' I said to Yorkie, resignedly.

Had I not been drunk I would have remembered a golden rule of fighting that our unarmed-combat instructor always told us: make sure you have the advantage. But, like a complete idiot, I walked straight out through that door. Not only had the hulk a few more seconds for his eyes to dilate, but he was against a black background and I was framed in the doorway's light!

I never felt a thing. I came to with Yorkie slapping the back of my hand and pleading with me to wake up.

I was covered with my own blood. My top lip had been split to almost its full length and was bleeding like a stuck pig. There was a huge lump behind my left ear and the bottom of my right rib cage hurt so much I could hardly breathe.

'He must have put the boot in,' I gasped.

'He did,' said Yorkie. 'Twice.'

'And what the hell were you doing?'

'I'm sorry, Kingy. I really am. And what could I do? I've never had a fight in my life.'

He helped me to my feet. 'For someone who doesn't fight,' I told him, 'you've certainly got a big mouth. You want to learn to keep it shut. Just look at my uniform! And where's that bastard now?'

206

'He's gone. He barged back into the bar, took no notice of me, thank God, and went straight out through the front door without drinking his beer or paying for it.'

I pushed his helping hand away. 'Pay the bill and get a taxi. I want to go to bed.'

'You sure you're OK? That lip's pretty bad. You should see the camp doctor. And you might have cracked ribs.'

'Sod the doctor,' I said. 'He'll only want to put a stitch in it, and my moustache will always hide the scar. I'm pretty sure, too, my ribs are only bruised.'

In the taxi, I said to Yorkie: 'It's times like this that I really miss the Paras. If I were still with them and this happened, the whole barrackroom would search the town for that Argyll and knock the living daylights out of him.'

The night before he was due to go to Kuala Lumpur, and after much persuasion, I agreed to have a last beer with Yorkie. We were sitting in an almost empty bar when three rowdy Malayans came in. Soon they were laughing and talking loudly, looking at us, saying something and laughing again.

Too late, I saw the Tiger-induced belligerence in Yorkie's eyes. Before I could do anything he leapt to his feet and yelled at the Malayans: 'Get stuffed! Fuck off, the lot of you!'

The laughter stopped and one Malayan instantly picked up a beer bottle and hurled it at us. Its neck snapped off as it hit the wall just behind us. My red temper flared. I picked up the neckless bottle and threw it at the fleeing Malayans. And the razor-sharp, ragged edge took the front part of my forefinger with it!

(Should that Argyll and Yorkie be reading this, I would like you to know that those two scars are still visible today. But, letting bygones be bygones, I would be more than happy to stand you both a drink.)

One morning, Fosty handed to me a very officious-looking Army form. 'Time you started thinking about what you are going to do when you leave the Army. It won't be long before you're going home. Fill this in and hand it in to the education department in the town centre.'

Fosty took a little cardboard box from his breast pocket. 'This is for you, too,' he added.

I opened it, and inside were the Malayan Star and ribbon. 'But I've never been anywhere near the fighting,' I exclaimed. 'All I've done is have a bloody cushy time, and I get a medal. It's an insult to those poor sods up in the jungle.'

He shrugged. 'It's official. Orders are orders and you are obliged to wear it. Get the ribbon sewn on straightaway. Singapore is classed as a theatre of war and you've been here three months.'

I'd been thinking a lot about what I was going to do after demob and, quite honestly, I didn't want to do anything! Life on an island, like the ones off Kure, really appealed, and that appeal continued, although submerged, for twenty-three years until it manifested itself and I acted upon it.

I felt truly upset as I sewed on the false medal ribbon; and I was most recalcitrant when I filled in the form. The largest Question/Answer panel wanted to know what profession I intended to follow and asked me to list two choices. Under First Choice, I wrote 'Hobo': and under the second, 'Knight of the road'!

A week later I appeared before an angry education major.

'I don't like insubordination one little bit, Kingsland,' he said. 'Now then, stop being an utter ass or I'll have you clapped in irons. *What* are you going to do? I'm here to help you.'

'I don't know, sir. I really don't.'

'Do you want to go back to farming?'

'No, sir. Definitely not.'

'What about electronics or teaching?'

Again a definite no.

'Do you want to sign on again?'

'I can't,' I said, and told him about my mother.

'Well, what the devil are you going to do, man? And don't tell me "Tramp" 'cos I won't tolerate it.'

I thought that this question-answer session was similar

to the joke where a soldier went to the medical officer with severe stomach pains. 'Have your bowels been open today?' asked the MO. 'No, sir, I wasn't issued with any.' 'No, no, no. Have you *passed* anything today?' 'A squad of men coming up the road, sir.' 'No, you fool, have you shit?' 'No, sir, I thought the stink was from you!'

But there was one profession that the sober, austere and military atmosphere of his office brought forward from the back of my mind:

'I think I would like to be a writer, sir.'

'Pah!' he snorted. 'You don't look like a writer, you don't act like a writer and you certainly don't talk like one.'

I often wondered afterwards how a writer was supposed to look, act and speak.

Unperturbed, I told him about my school essay and the article that the *Bucks Advertiser* had published.

He thought for several moments. 'I would like to see that article,' he said. Next day I took it to him.

'Yes,' he said, after reading it. 'You certainly have a descriptive flair. Do you think the editor would be prepared to take you on as a reporter?'

'I don't know, sir.'

'Well, let's find out, shall we? I'll get a letter off to him straightaway.'

It was two weeks before I was told that the education major wanted to see me again.

'I've had a letter from Mr How,' he said. 'Naturally he would like to see and talk to you first, but he would be able to take you on as what is termed an adult entrant into journalism provided you are willing to accept a lower salary until you are trained.'

'That's really good of him. Thank you, sir.'

He looked at the letter in front of him. 'However,' he continued, 'there is another proviso – because of union rules he cannot accept you unless you are able to type and have a good shorthand speed.'

Very disappointed, I told him: 'Well, that puts the lid on that. I've never touched a typewriter and I don't think I've ever seen shorthand.'

The major smiled. 'No,' he said, 'it hasn't put the lid on it. I don't think I've told you this but because of your service in Korea you are eligible for a bounty.'

'Am I really?' I asked, greatly surprised and pleased. 'I thought it was only mercenaries who got that sort of thing.'

He coughed. 'Just take my word for it. You have an excellent war record – apart from a final blemish – naughty of you to sleep on guard – but the bounty will not be in the form of a lump cash sum. What we are prepared to do is this: pay for you to attend a technical college for six months where you will take English at Higher National Certificate level and learn shorthand-typing. Your lodgings will be paid and you will receive an adequate pocket allowance. So what do you say? Agreed?'

'Yes, sir!'

'Good! Now let's fill in this form correctly.'

22

The voyage home to Southampton, on the fast troopship *Empire Fowie*, holds only three memories for me. The first and most lengthy one was after we had passed by India. Suddenly it was Christmas Eve and I was asked if I would MC and play the records for an officers' dance on the upper deck.

The sea was as flat as a pancake, the air was balmy and the stars were big, bright and romantic. As the evening lengthened into night so did a long line of drink bribes. 'I say, old chap, this is for you. Would you play the "Waltz of the Toreadors"?' – or such and such a record. The 'this is for you' was anything from whisky to beer. But I drank with discrimination, because I had designs on a sweet young thing with enormous tits who kept staring at me as she danced with her drunken husband.

Shortly after midnight, hubby decided to prove he had had enough by throwing up over the side, and sweet young thing put him to bed. She returned and became joint MC. When the dance ended in the early hours, the lights went out and we were alone. Within minutes we were hotly engaged in a knee trembler at the rail.

'I feel absolutely disgusted with myself,' she said afterwards. 'Your stuff has run down and soaked my stockings.' Ten minutes later we had another knee trembler! When I met her again two days later, she looked right through me . . .

The next two memories are close together. Trouble had hit Suez and the giant statue of de Lesseps was pitched on its head in the water. So much for him, I thought. The Mediterranean was choppy and produced a pronounced roll.

A few hours later I was sitting in the bar, drinking a pint

and watching the porthole dip below the waterline and shoot up again. Without warning, seasickness struck. How strange, I thought, that after weathering a storm in the *Unicorn*'s galley I should succumb to a mere choppy sea.

February isn't the best of months to arrive in England, especially from the Tropics. But, despite the cold, I loved her and kept my eyes steadfastly on her wintered scenes as the train took me from Southampton to London. Now and then I felt that I hadn't really been away at all; that I hadn't really seen, done and endured all those things. Everybody and everything looked the same. No one knew about the excitement and happiness bubbling inside me. I had returned a hero only in my own eyes.

'I'm back! I'm back!' I wanted to shout. 'Look at my war ribbons!'

But the faces of ticket collectors and people were lugubrious, reserved, cold and drawn. It was not until I phoned Mum from Woolwich that I encountered jubilation. She screeched with delight and started crying. Geoff had to take the phone from her so that I could tell them I would be demobbed in three days' time and would phone again when I knew the exact time of the train. That night I slept the blissful sleep of the dead.

Next day was filled with form-filling, kit checks and the issue of a demob suit. I was also handed a pink slip of paper that entitled me, without any test, to a civilian driving licence. That night I went to a pub I remembered for its liveliness and whores. It was empty. Nine o'clock arrived and still I was the only one there.

'Where is everybody tonight?' I asked the landlord.

'Television, mate.' He looked at my ribbons and the fading yellowy tan on my face and the backs of my hands. 'Been out of the country, eh? So you wouldn't know. Everybody's gone television crazy. Killed pub life completely. They are all sitting at home watching a bloody square box.'

A blonde of about thirty-five came in at ten o'clock when I was sipping my eleventh black and tan. After drinking Tiger it was like drinking water – probably was – and all it did was make me empty my bladder every twenty minutes or so.

The blonde, smartly dressed in a tailored beige coat and skirt under a full-length beaver lamb, sat on the bar stool next to mine and showed me a generous length of stockinged thigh and a pink nylon slip. I bought her brandy and peppermint until closing time and she accommodated me at the rear of the pub against the urinal's wall.

On the day I was demobbed I found she had given me a dose of crabs! How terribly ironic, I thought, after all those women I had associated with in the Far East.

And those irritating mites became part of the glory I arrived home to Aylesbury with. Mum, Geoff – with Muriel, his wife of a few months – and Tania were waiting on the platform as, itching like mad, I stepped down from the train.

Tania went into hysterical barking and tried to eat me, Mum burst into tears and tried to hug me, Geoff was pumping my hand and Muriel was smiling and waiting to kiss me. It was all too much. I cried, too, and it felt as though the tears were washing away all the pent-up fear and Korean soil once and for all. Then I was calm and happy – and we were all talking at the same time.

I confided in Geoff about the crabs. 'Vinegar,' he said. 'That will kill them.' It did, too, though it took a couple of days. Once or twice Mum remarked: 'I can't understand it. There seems to be a strong smell of vinegar in the bathroom.'

For a week I was treated like the prodigal son. I did the rounds, visiting friends, relations and near-empty pubs. And almost every night, like a ritual, was television.

My interview with Johnny How was successful and he looked forward to seeing me in October. My course at Slough Tech wasn't to start until April. Gradually I became bored with doing nothing, and I always felt cold. I began yearning for the heat and social life of Singapore. In comparison, Aylesbury was like a morgue. Also, I felt strangely insecure without the protection the Army had given me and I missed the company of men. Several times I almost decided to re-enlist. Mum was all right. Geoff had his own electrical business and he had bought the house, and Mum and Muriel were the best of friends.

But I knew that I didn't really want to go back into the Army. I had been offered a future in a respectable and oft-thought romantic profession. Not bad for a former straw-sucking hick! And Mum was very proud of me.

At last the day arrived for me to go to Slough and start a new and different life. About a week beforehand I'd had the first of what was to become a bad series of terrible nightmares. They always ended with the first man I had shot cutting my stomach to pieces with a machine-gun. The nightmares became so severe that I was forced to seek medical and psychiatric aid.

But that, of course, like the new career that was to take me to Fleet Street, then into the world of sex magazines, to wine growing in Italy and, finally, to the life of an adventurer, is another story.

Who knows? Perhaps one day I might even write it.